THE FALCON GUIDE TO

VAN LIFE

every essential for nomadic adventures

BEN AND ROXY DAWSON

FALCONGUIDES®

Guilford, Connecticut

FALCONGUIDES®

An imprint of The Rowman & Littlefield Publishing Group, Inc.
4501 Forbes Blvd., Ste. 200
Lanham, MD 20706
www.rowman.com

Falcon and FalconGuides are registered trademarks and Make Adventure Your Story is a trademark of The Rowman & Littlefield Publishing Group, Inc.

Distributed by NATIONAL BOOK NETWORK

British Library Cataloguing-in-Publication Information available

Library of Congress Cataloging-in-Publication Data available

ISBN 978-1-4930-5907-2 (paper : alk. paper)
ISBN 978-1-4930-5908-9 (electronic)

♾™ The paper used in this publication meets the minimum requirements of American National Standard for Information Sciences—Permanence of Paper for Printed Library Materials, ANSI/NISO Z39.48-1992.

CONTENTS

INTRODUCTION

SINCE WE LIFTED OUR CHESTS AND PUT ONE FOOT in front of the other, humans have been on the move. It's only recently in the scheme of human existence (ten thousand years in the two-hundred-thousand-year story of humankind) that we have set down roots and watched the sunrise from the same familiar plot of land each new day. When early humans began settling down, periods of movement were interspersed with months of shelter and community building. As they say, "Home is where the food is," so humans were always ready to pick everything up, wrap it in a blanket, and sling it over their shoulders to look for greener pastures. That may be an exaggeration—we're sure our early human ancestors had much more efficient ways of carrying their things than a bindle. Nonetheless, the transition to a stationary lifestyle wasn't easy. Now, ten thousand years later, many modern humans still struggle with static circumstances, both physically and mentally. A primal call echoes in the back of many of our minds: Head for the open road, resist roots, seek adventure, pursue novel experiences. The life of a nomad has evolved over the millennia along with technology and mode of transportation.

Long before there was an application that supported hashtags and clever portmanteaus, dedicated nomads covered unfathomable distances in search of resources, opportunity, salvation, or simply escape. Caravans of humans accompanied by thousands of camels made the dangerous passage across the Sahara (which was then more forest than desert). #Camellife morphed into #wagonlife in the 1800s. The Romani people were known for traveling as free nomads in round wagons, called vardos, across Europe. The vardo was intricately painted, carved, and often had chimneys and large wheels on the outside. The Romani people originated in northwestern India in 500 CE and still travel today, with large populations in the United States and Brazil. Their official flag boasts a large wagon wheel, an homage to their traveling ways. #Wagonlife found its way to the United States in the form of Conestoga Wagons in the 1700s that were used for migrating south through the Appalachian Valley. Once the automobile hit the scene, there was no stopping #vanlife. Thomas Hiram Holding started the Caravan Club in 1907, its aim, to ". . . bring together those interested in van life as a pastime . . . to improve and supply suitable vans and other appliances . . . and to arrange camping grounds." The United States' national pastime, autocamping, was enjoyed by Thomas Edison, Henry Ford, and

Theodore Roosevelt (who was known to conduct political business, like conservation of federal lands, from the mosquito-filled wilderness).

Finally, the iconic Volkswagen Splitscreen (named for the split down the windshield) was released in 1950. Known by many names—Splittie, Microbus, Volkswagen Type 2, hippie mobile, hippie van—this vehicle became synonymous with the counterculture hippie movement of the 1960s. The Westy (Westfalia) also became a popular choice, donning surfboards hanging from the sides and acoustic guitars stacked on the seats. Van life has seeped into modern culture. If we had a gallon of gas for every time someone responded to "I live in a van," with the iconic words from SNL's Chris Farley, "I am thirty-five years old, I am divorced, and I live in a van down by the river!" we could drive to the tip of Argentina without stopping. Now that van life is fully in the mainstream, there are so many different types of vans on the market, creative and unique conversions, and equally creative and unique humans living in them.

Discontent is on the rise in the sedentary lives of twenty-first-century Americans. Studies show that people are less happy than forty years ago (and most likely ten thousand years ago). Doctors prescribe antidepressants at four hundred times the rate that they

did twenty years ago. It's hard to pinpoint exactly what has caused the decline in mental health. Maybe having our faces drawn to the unsympathetic glow of a smartphone instead of the intimate hills on the horizon? Or maybe it's because human interaction is now mostly done through ones and zeroes over the internet with the protection of anonymity and lack of vulnerability or connection.

These modern situations grow the ball of anxiety nestled at the base of your rib cage. And these things become smaller parts of the routine after completely changing your lifestyle and moving into a van full-time. Nothing like the panic-inducing but simple "No service" replacing the status bars at the top of your phone to physically and mentally signal you to put your attention elsewhere. Move away from the blue light and toward the circle of other nomads situated around the fire. Relax, breathe in the crisp, dry night air, and focus on the now.

The notion of hitting the open road and driving into the sunset sounds romantic, adventurous, and straight-up cool. "The adventure is simply existing," an exhilarating—yet

simple—slogan. The scenery just outside the window speeds by while the big picture on the horizon ambles along. New humans rotate in and out, popping up again down the road. Your backyard is massive. Rock climb in the morning, float a river that evening, have a drink by the fire at the end of the day, and then do it all again the next day. Mountain bike to the coffee shop in town for some Wi-Fi. Sleep at the trailhead and be the first person to the summit the next morning. The possibilities span out in front of you in all directions. A van is, at any given moment, at a metaphorical intersection with one thousand roads leading in every direction. It's both terrifying and freeing at the same time.

There are so many different kinds of days. Living in a van, they don't begin with the same old morning commute to sit under fluorescent lights for eight hours. We make our own schedule, work from anywhere with Wi-Fi, and see each day's sunset or sunrise (and sometimes both). Read all of this with caution, though. It ain't easy. In between those morning mountain-bike rides and evening campfires are flat tires, misread maps, and so many dishes.

Over the years of living nomadically, full-time from a van, we've heard the phrases "Oh, I've always dreamt of doing that" and "I wish I did that when I was younger" an incalculable number of times. But what are the steps to get the rubber to the pavement? Have all those people who said to us "I've always wanted to do that" moved into a van? Most likely, no. We want this guide to help you get closer to a yes. It is possible to completely change your life, channel your inner Neanderthal, and move into a home on wheels.

We are Ben and Roxy. We've been living in a van full-time since 2017. We began our nomadic journey as the road team for *Elevation Outdoors and Blue Ridge Outdoors* magazines and have been jumping from one traveling job to another ever since. We are writers, photographers, and wife and husband. Most of our relationship has been spent on the road. Another phrase we hear all the time? "If you can make it together in a van, you're set." We guess it's true!

After living in a company-provided van for eight months, we decided to purchase and build out our own high-roof van and use it as our home and our work vehicle full-time. After living in a van that was converted by somebody else, we had a great foundation for how we'd like to build out our own van.

As you flip through this book, you'll notice that we're occasionally driving different vans. Over the past years, we've traveled through various countries, renting vans when we land and experiencing different cultures and road signs from a new-to-us home on wheels. You'll also notice a lot of logos on our different vans throughout the book. All of the logos pictured are from using our van as a work vehicle. We would allow our clients to wrap the van in graphics while we were under contract. We promise we're not trying to sell you anything.

I, Roxy, grew up in northern Virginia, in a sprawling suburb of Washington, D.C. There were strip malls, box stores, and crowded highways. It was a great place to grow up but not a great place to feel free and fully realized (which I'm still working on). When my world grew from my house to the mall to the city a metro ride away, it dawned on my eighteen-year-old self that there was far more beyond the melted asphalt and polluted sunsets. I left for New York City (which, looking back, was just more melted asphalt and polluted sunsets) to attend NYU for film production and music. I stayed in New York City for six full years, which, from on top of the fluffy comforter in the back of my van, with the doors swung open

and the breeze picking up, feels like an eternity. A different Roxy lived in that city. After six years I moved to Colorado, and after three years of spending as much time beyond the front range as possible, I moved into a van full-time. The path was linear, in the sense that I went from one extreme in New York City, passed through the middle with an apartment, roommates, and a day job, and ended up at the other end: full-time nomadic living. I was taking baby steps the whole time, not realizing the end goal. Moving from a major city, paring down my things. Living in Colorado, realizing the outdoors was a key to happiness. I am currently house-less, living full-time from the van, relying on friends and family for mailing addresses, showers (when it's freezing), and sometimes a guest bed. I can honestly say my brain chemistry has changed for the better.

I, Ben, grew up in Cincinnati, Ohio. For as long as I can remember, I've loved being outside. Growing up in the suburbs, I found my love for nature and the outdoors in the dense midwestern woods. I spent my summers catching frogs and tadpoles in an algae-covered pond behind my parents' house. I came home covered in mud every single day. In July I spent humid evenings watching the lightning bugs in the tall grassy fields down the street.

I stayed in Cincinnati for college and studied audio-video production. During this time my love for the outdoors took a backseat to my desk job and stayed that way for a couple of years. Sometime in 2013, ready for a change, I moved to Colorado. Once I moved, my desire to experience nature and the Rocky Mountains became more intense by the day. Once Roxy and I met, it wasn't long before we were going on road trips every single weekend. Soon, weekends just weren't enough for us. We started looking for remote jobs, with the intention to hit the road for as long as possible. Our search continued until we lucked out big time.

This book is intended to support your exploration. Readers will (hopefully!) come away with a deeper knowledge of how to live happily and wholly in a vehicle, and explore the opportunity to connect more closely and experience more fully the wonders these beautiful lands offer. We respectfully acknowledge that this book covers the traditional land of Native peoples. Native-Land.ca is a valuable resource that informed specific traditional land acknowledgments in this book and is a comprehensive guide for explorers to learn more about the Native and ancestral stewards of this land that we love. It is also

a work in progress. Acknowledgments listed in this book do not represent official or legal boundaries.

Thank you to all our friends and family (incredible editors in this family—Reade, we are eternally grateful!) and van life contributors for offering advice, help, time, and support throughout the writing of this guidebook. We are eternally grateful, and this guidebook wouldn't have been completed without your help. Thank you.

SCOTT HARDESTY

DREAM + PREPARE

chapter 1 DEFINING THE DREAM

WHAT IS VAN LIFE?

WE'VE ALL SEEN THE PERFECTLY ARRANGED PILLOWS, the half-clothed twenty-something laying on them, and the two back doors swung open to a pristine enchanting wilderness backdrop. It's a common image as you scroll through Instagram dreaming of a nomadic lifestyle. While that may be a reality for a small percentage of van lifers (or 0 percent), the truth of van life is far from that carefully composed picture. Similar to all adventurous lifestyles, it has big ups, big downs, and quick swings between them.

Van life is nomadic living. It is sleeping on four wheels just for now or forever, on the road to grand adventures. Van life can include vehicles as small as the Nissan Cube and as large as a school bus. They can be home for one night out of the year or 365.

Along our journey we have run into van dwellers of all ages. From families with young children and teenagers to solo older women to couples and friends. There is no age

requirement for van life (although a driver's license helps), only the desire to live the life-style, whatever that may be.

There are so many ways to live van life. There are those that use their van for week-end excursions—"weekenders." Some choose to live full-time in their van, giving up any other form of permanent housing and relying solely on their van as shelter—"full-timers." Others live in their van seasonally, for example, spending winters on the Baja Peninsula and working through summers while living in a permanent residence. This book is writ-ten as a guide for a life of travel. Cost-of-living expenses are limited in a van, but it's still a luxury. We're grateful for the freedom to be untethered and spend our days in pursuit of adventure.

It is popular among van life communities to camp in fair weather. This is advanta-geous for many reasons. Without a heater, it is best to stay in warmer climates so you are comfortable at night. One of the big draws of van life is to experience the great outdoors. The area where you are parked essentially becomes your backyard. Following warmer

RANDI & STEVE HITCHCOCK

RANDI AND STEVE TRAVEL AS A FAMILY WITH THEIR SON, CODY, in their Ford E350. They crawl up weather-beaten washes in Utah in search of arrowheads (to photograph, never take), and play bocce on whatever terrain their van happens to be parked on that evening. They've recently made the switch from van life to boat life to expand their exploring to the wide-open seas.

VEHICLE + WHY
2006 Ford E350 Cargo Van—it was diesel, had an extended body, and parts are readily available.

2002 Fountaine Pajot Athena 38-foot boat—we wanted a galley-up model, right around 40 feet and within our price range.

CONNECT
@van_humboldt, @destination_adrift

TIME ON THE ROAD
Part-time, 8 years

TRAVELING AS A FAMILY
Get to know one another *really* well before you head out for a long period of time. It's a very different situation in a van than when everyone has a separate room to go to, or electronics to "check out" with. You're in it together . . . literally. All. The. Time. Pack lots of "unplugged" activities (small games like a deck of cards or a mini chess set) so that you have backup if you get bored. Take *lots* of outdoor toys (as long as they fit) that you'll use often. For instance, our son's snorkel gear keeps him occupied for *hours* at a lake or beach and hardly takes up any space.

WORDS OF WISDOM
My husband and I love it! My son would probably not say the same, but as long as he can "plug in" sometimes and access Wi-Fi, he's okay (and actually does have fun when we kick him off or he can't connect). We have created quite a special family bond. We delegate tasks that each person does to help set up/tear down camp, and even have many more fun traditions now that we are not bound to city life (such as camping out during full moons and howling). At times, it's trying . . . it's a small space for three adult-sized people and two dogs.

climate trends expands your backyard options and ability to recreate outdoors. There are also some van lifers who follow colder temperatures and snowstorms, looking for the best skiing and winter sport conditions. This guidebook focuses on North America's camping areas and both warm and cold weather.

One of the biggest questions about van life is how to make money. The short answer is technology and creativity. A lot of work doesn't require office space, giving rise to the "digital nomad." A digital nomad is anyone who works remotely while traveling. There is a growing trend of remote work in the United States, as well as a growing trend of employers offering remote work options. Almost every coffee shop offers free Wi-Fi with a purchase and most libraries offer free internet (and many other services like printing if needed). While pay is usually lower, living in a van also lowers your expenses. If you are full-time, you don't have rent or utilities. You often shop less, order less, make more of your own food, and generally have less stuff to maintain and replace. Being a digital nomad requires a functioning laptop and skills that can transfer to online work. We know many van lifers who run other types of business from the road, including selling jewelry, paintings, and other homemade hard goods. Some van lifers house-sit and pet-sit for extra cash. With lowered expenses, there are many avenues to make ends meet.

COLIN BOYD & SOFI ALDINIO

COLIN AND SOFI TRAVEL WITH THEIR TWO YOUNG BOYS in a mystical, orange Mercedes.

VEHICLE + WHY
1978 Mercedes 508D German Command & Control Vehicle—the universe delivered it to us.

CONNECT
@AfueraVida

COLIN BOYD & SOFI ALDINIO

TIME ON THE ROAD
Full-time, a year and a half

LEAVING
Travel and experience have guided our spirits since a young age and both of us felt a deep desire to share this with our children. However, our life leading up to van life looked a lot like those who are likely reading this guide. A full-time nine-to-five job, a full-time parenting role, scheduled weekends, a fragile marriage, increasing expenses always leaving little money in the bank, and a whole lot of commitments in our life that we did not consciously sign up for.

The inspiration for us was to shirk this lifestyle and embark on a journey that would reignite our spirit of adventure and cast our family on a new collective journey together.

TRAVELING AS A FAMILY
As a father I've gone from having four hours a day with my boys to twenty-four, which was one of the hardest but most rewarding adjustments to make.

It's been the best decision we've ever made to do this together. Our bond is tighter. We guide our kids' values and education every day, and they show us how to be present and grateful for the little things. But it's not all butterflies and rainbows—we've faced hell together, cried together, bled together—but that's the growth edge we sought out. While it has worked for us, we do not recommend this type of experience to any other family unless they really have a penchant for suffering.

WHY PURSUE VAN LIFE?

Why even hit the road to begin with? On our travels we have chatted with so many humans about their reasons to leave their apartment, sell most of their material posses- sions, and drive toward the sunset. Often it's discontent—a feeling that something just doesn't fit with their current situation. Some of our friends have had incredible jobs, great places to live, wonderful communities, and still felt something was missing. When they tell their friends or family they're leaving it all to live in a van, they're answered with, "That's impossible," or "Your life is so great." Others are enchanted by the romantic notion of living without roots. Some want the ability to travel long-term without relying on hotels or tent camping. There are thousands of reasons to hit the road.

PROTIP

When you tell someone your plans to start a new lifestyle, and they are excited for you, keep coming back to them for encouragement.

Balancing out those thousands of reasons, there are just as many legitimate excuses that make van life impossible for some. But often those excuses can be transformed into bumps in the road on your journey to living the life you want. Hopefully, this guidebook can get you multiple steps closer to van life, changing the "I've always wanted to" to "I am living my dream in a van."

PROTIP

Always remember that you can return back to the "normal" world at any time. You can go back to the nine-to-five, move into an apartment, and start again. This life-style change doesn't have to be permanent.

CHASE & MARIAJOSÉ

CHASE AND MARIAJOSÉ MADE THE LEAP to the nomadic lifestyle when Chase was affected by a corporate restructure. He was no longer employed and took a severance payout for ten years of service to his company. They were keen to find the biggest school bus they could, considering they were downsizing from a two-thousand+-square-foot house and wanted the largest possible floor plan to work with. After a few years they've downsized again and are building out a van.

VEHICLE + WHY
2016 Mercedes Sprinter 170" non-ext 2500 3.0L V6—we wanted a late-model Sprinter, used, but still in pristine condition.

CONNECT
@tioaventuravan | youtube.com/tíoaventura

TIME ON THE ROAD
Full-time, 2 years

MAKING THE LEAP
The largest reason we considered changing our life as much as we did was due to the gnawing thought that we were complacent with a life that left us unfulfilled.

Our biggest fears about leaving our "regular" lifestyle were the uncertainty of where we would go, where we would stay, and if we were making the right decision as a whole. We worried about comforts at first, which is why we planned a layout that was maximized for off-grid comfort, a large fridge, a large water tank (but realizing later one hundred gallons isn't even enough). We were also concerned about the process of decluttering, downsizing, and thinking a lot more consciously about things we had never truly taken into consideration.

Once you move into a van, the world rolls open. The entire continent becomes your outdoor playground. The obstacles of long drives, expensive hotels, and limited vacation time crumble. In a van you can park right outside a national park, head in at sunrise, explore for an entire day, and still be minutes from home as the sun blinks out its final rays. You can wake up on the beach, in a redwood forest, by a lake, or among mountains. You can cook dinner with a view of Monument Valley, hike from your doorstep, view wildlife from your front seat, and have dessert by the fire. We have experienced more in the past few years than we did for the decade before living nomadically. It is with our full hearts that we suggest, if you have any inkling this lifestyle is for you, you should pursue it with all you have. It has changed us as humans for the better, opened our arms to a new community, and grounded us to the earth in ways we never imagined.

chapter 2 BUILDING A BUDGET

HOW MUCH DOES VAN LIFE REALLY COST? What are the limiting factors and barriers to entry? Can you save money by living in a van? In this chapter we will set out sample budgets and provide you with a worksheet to create your own budget. This planning will help you get one step closer to the dirt roads and sandy campsites your heart desires. Major budget considerations are centered around the van itself, the build, and your month-to-month expenses on the road. Having a better understanding of these categories will give you a better idea of how much money to save in advance, what remote work to look for, and how much you actually need financially to make this lifestyle work. Over the next several chapters, we will go into detail on all three of these topics. Feel free to skip around as you make your own budget, grabbing more information when you need it from the chapters that follow.

It may be helpful to create a budget for your van + repairs (if purchasing an older vehicle) + build-out separately from your month-to-month (or weekend-to-weekend) budget of living in the vehicle.

VEHICLE COSTS

A large part of your van life budget is your vehicle. This can be the biggest upfront cost, depending on which type of vehicle and conversion method you choose. Below is a list of options and considerations. These are expanded on in chapter 3.

VEHICLE CONSIDERATIONS
- Space and height requirements
- Van family size
- Sleeping arrangements and needs
- Four-wheel drive vs. two-wheel drive
- Front-wheel drive vs. rear-wheel drive
- Towing capacity
- Gas mileage

TYPES OF VANS ON THE MARKET
- Class B motorhomes
- Professional van conversions
- Self-build in empty shell
- Used vehicle with preexisting build

COST OF A VEHICLE

Calculate how much you can realistically spend on a vehicle (leaving room for planned conversion costs), and start your search in that price range. Alternatively, you can cut things from your conversion to get a pricier vehicle and know you will be adding to the build down the line. You will likely have to perform maintenance on whatever vehicle you choose. Even new vehicles will need oil changes and new tires from time to time.

Alternatively you can purchase a used vehicle for less and know you will be spending money on repairs. Choosing your van is all about what's important to you, your vision for the future, and your current resources. The process looks a little different for everyone. A long conversion timeline is one way to disperse expenses and maintain your stationary home and regular income while completing your build. This approach worked well for the couple profiled on page 14. The van was on their schedule, and they didn't hit the road until it was ready to roll. If you're on a tight and unforgiving schedule, you're forced into a more hurried timeline.

COST OF MAINTENANCE

Costs associated with vehicle maintenance are just a part of van life. Even if you don't break down, you'll have ongoing vehicle maintenance including oil changes, tires, brakes, etc. An oil change for a midsized van will range anywhere from around $35 for a standard oil change to around $100 if you use full-synthetic oil. Most new vans have oil change sensors to indicate when an oil change is needed. If you don't have an oil change indicator, you can consult your owner's manual for details on oil change intervals. Most newer-vehicle oil change intervals range between every five thousand and ten thousand miles or every six months, whichever comes first. Older vehicles might have an oil change interval of three thousand miles. Every thirty thousand to fifty thousand miles or so, depending on a lot of factors, you may need to replace tires and brakes. You can expect to pay anywhere between about $600 and $1,200 for tires depending on type and quality. Brakes are another item that you'll have to eventually replace. Large cargo vans use beefy brakes and they can be costly. It's a good idea to budget around $1,000 for a full brake job to be done by a mechanic. That might be a little high, but it's better to budget a little extra than fall short. Consider keeping a vehicle maintenance fund of around $2,000 just in case you have a maintenance issue. Your vehicle costs are now home costs.

NATALIE & ABIGAIL

NATALIE AND ABIGAIL WERE CRAVING A CHANGE IN LIFE. The "normal" nine-to-five wasn't fulfilling them. A desire for travel and to live intentionally and minimally led them to the nomadic lifestyle.

VEHICLE + WHY
2004 Sprinter Van, high-top, 21 feet long—we just wanted a vehicle we could stand up in.

CONNECT
@letsplayrideandseek

TIME ON THE ROAD
Full-time, 1½ years

MAKING THE LEAP
A lot of planning and time went into moving into a van. We started saving money a few months before searching for a van. After purchasing the van, it took us one and a half years to build it out while we were working full-time. Neither of us had any building experience so that was a huge challenge for us. We didn't set out looking for a Sprinter, we just wanted a vehicle we could stand up in. While searching, we came across this one for sale at a towing company. It used to be a prisoner transport vehicle and now it is our personal freedom vehicle. We chose a van over an RV because we wanted a vehicle we could drive safely, that would fit in a parking spot, and that we could make into a cozy home.

BUILD-OUT CONSIDERATIONS

Unless you plan to buy a rig that's already built out, factor in an estimated cost of build-out while looking around for a vehicle. It's hard to imagine the build-out before actually seeing the physical vehicle, but having a ballpark number in mind will help you out enormously down the line. We've heard plenty of horror stories of people paying as they go, without a budget to follow, and running out of funds halfway through the build. Getting caught with nothing left in your budget while building the bed platform or cabinets is one thing, but if you run out of funds halfway through your plumbing, you're going to be sad, and probably wet. Building your budget can start with designing your build (and it's fun!). To get into the nitty-gritty of starting your own build, head to chapter 4, where we detail and explain almost everything you would want to put in your home on wheels.

PROTIP

Plan on heading to the hardware store several times a week, if not several times in a day. Some van lifers even work on their vehicle in the parking lot of the hardware store to save on gas.

SAMPLE BUILD-OUTS FROM VAN LIFERS IN THIS BOOK

WHO	WHAT	VEHICLE PRICE	BUILD PRICE	TOTAL
Chris Stephan	2008 Jeep Grand Cherokee	Already owned, $0	$400	$400
LeeAnn Juday	1984 GMC Vandura, original interior build	$500 purchase, $3,200 mechanical repair cost	$0, original build was intact with fold-out bed	$3,700
LeeAnn Juday (second vehicle)	1996 Ford Work Van	$2,000 purchase, $400 mechanical repair cost	$1,700	$4,100
Dani Reyes-Acosta	1995 Ford E250 RWD	$4,300	$2,000	$6,300
Scott Woerner	E350 van	$2,700	$6,000	$8,700
Scott & Cassie	2005 Chevy Astro	$2,800 (with $4,000 in two separate defective transmission repairs)	$2,000	$8,800
Katya	2012 Ford Transit Connect	$9,300	$2,500	$11,800
Laura Edmondson	2013 Ford Transit Connect	$11,000	$4,000	$15,000
Chase & Mariajosé	Skoolie			$16,000
Natalie & Abigail	2004 Sprinter Van, high top	$6,000	$10,000	$16,000
Connie Shang	Red 2003 Freightliner Sprinter	Owned by parent, $10,000 for repairs	$10,000	$20,000
Brandon & Gabi Fox	1972 Airstream Overlander	$6,500	$20,000	$26,500
Charlie Mertens	2004 Chevy Express AWD with a high top	$8,000	$20,000	$28,000
Chase & Mariajosé	2016 Mercedes Sprinter 170"	$18,300	$10,000 (and counting)	$28,000
Sydney Ferbrache	2017 Ford Transit High Roof	$24,000 (financed)	$10,000	$34,000
Roxy & Ben	2018 Ram ProMaster High Roof FWD	$30,000 (purchased new, making monthly payments of $600)	$7,000	$37,000
Colin Boyd & Sofi Aldinio	1978 Mercedes 508D German Command & Control Vehicle	$30,000	$10,000	$40,000
Randi & Steve Hitchcock	Ford E350, diesel	$12,000—later had to pay $22,000 for new motor and transmission after five years of owning it	$8,000	$42,000
Derek Redd	2018 Mercedes-Benz Sprinter	$40,000 (purchased new)	$20,000	$60,000

WHO WILL DO THE WORK?

HIRING A PROFESSIONAL

- High experience level
- Often comes with warranty
- Can combine with van purchase and have one large loan

BUILD IT YOURSELF

- Intimate knowledge of your build
- Personal touches
- Ability to fix problems as they arise

ELEMENTS TO CONSIDER

- Insulation
- Vents, air circulation, and awnings
- Auxiliary power and solar power
- Heaters

- Fresh water and gray water
- Showers
- Camp toilets
- Cabinetry

LAYOUT

Social media platforms can be a great place to get creative ideas for layout recommendations, measurements, and plans. A conversion can be as simple as throwing an air mattress on the floor and using a Jetboil to cook (low cost and build time), or as complex as building a shower and toilet behind the driver's seat (high cost, maintenance, and build time).

VAN AND BUILD BUDGET CONSIDERATION SUMMARY

- Cost of purchasing a vehicle that you do not already own
- Cost of insuring a vehicle that is not already insured (Some vehicles cost more to insure than others.)
- Cost and time spent searching for the correct vehicle
- Cost of vehicle registration and inspections for older vehicles (In states like Colorado, newer cars cost more to register.)
- Build cost (total cost of the build including all tools, materials, and hired help)
- Vehicle maintenance and safety upgrades
- Gas mileage (applies to living budget, but important to consider while purchasing)
- Cost of dismantling the interior of a used vehicle

LIVING BUDGET

A month-to-month living budget is incredibly personal. You could live on less than $1,000 a month, or spend far, far more. You can stay in national park campgrounds, eat canned beans for breakfast, or both. You can drive cross country twice in a month, or stay put in a free site off of a backroad, only moving to re-up on groceries. Oftentimes, nomads choose to move into a van to save money on rent. A van payment is usually much lower than rent, and you will be saving on utilities, but there are many other expenses to examine. Below are categories to consider in your month-to-month expenses and a sample of what one month might look like.

INCOMING MONEY

- Penny pinching (and saving) beforehand and living off those savings
- Full-time, part-time, contract work
- Remote work for the company you currently work for
- Starting your own business from the road
- Seasonal work
- Farm stays, WWOOFing (World Wide Opportunities on Organic Farms)
- City-specific work, staying in one place and completing a few jobs, then moving on

OUTGOING MONEY: VAN

- Automobile insurance
- Van payment
- Build-out payment
- Gas
- Maintenance

ON-THE-ROAD COSTS AND CONSIDERATIONS—TWO PEOPLE

OUTGOING MONEY: VAN	NOTES	MONTHLY COST	SAVING STRATEGIES
Automobile insurance	USAA	$104	—
Van payment (if purchased new)	2018 Ram ProMaster	$607	—
Build-out payment (if a third party was used)	No loan, paid in full	—	—
Gas	Medium-movement month	$280	Move around less frequently
Maintenance	Oil change	$35	—
	Van total:	$1,026	
OUTGOING MONEY: PERSONAL			
Health Insurance	Colorado Marketplace, 2 people	$185	—
Groceries/alcohol/eating out	Groceries, bottle of Mezcal, and wine	$450	More intentional meal planning
Water and/or ice (depending on your setup)	Fridge	—	—
Campgrounds	Camped on public land	—	—
Experiences	National Parks Pass	$80	Pass is good for the whole year
Telephone, internet	Separate family plans	$130	Work at cafes
Laundry	At friends' houses	—	—
Gym membership/showers	Use solar shower	—	—
Entertainment subscriptions	Netflix, Spotify	$21	Rely on free services
Gifts, clothing, gear	Miscellaneous	$100	Fewer national park pins!
Toll roads	Routed around	—	—
Emergency	Put away $ every month	$100	—
AAA coverage	Family plan	$11	—
Pet supplies and food	Dog food	$40	—
	Personal Total:	$1,117	
	Total monthly expenses:	$2,143	

OUTGOING MONEY: PERSONAL

- Groceries/alcohol/eating out
- Water and/or ice (depending on your setup)
- Health insurance
- Campgrounds
- Experiences
- Telephone, internet
- Laundry
- Gym membership/showers
- School materials, toys, activities for children
- Entertainment subscriptions
- Gifts, clothing, gear
- Toll roads
- Emergency fund
- AAA coverage
- Pet supplies and food

Most people who are interested in moving into a van are intrigued by simplifying. This may accompany lowering your budget as well. Below we will highlight some ways to keep your budget low while traveling.

GAS

This is one of the biggest expenses and one of the easiest to alleviate. Find a beautiful spot, and stay put. Driving across the country is expensive. Driving down the coast is expensive. Staying in one place is *mostly* free. If you can find an internet connection and a legal spot on public land and you have the freedom to take it slow, do it! It is a wonderful way to get to know the area and also save money.

HEALTH INSURANCE

This can be an extremely tricky topic depending on your work situation and home state. In the United States, health insurance is tied to your employment, and moving to a contract or freelance work situation can mean a big hit in your budget to pay personal insurance. This can get even more complicated with children.

It is helpful to talk to an insurance broker in your home state to see what the options are. You can also look into health-share plans, and short-term medical plans if you don't plan on traveling long-term. Another option is telemedicine plans that can be used throughout the country. We both have insurance through the Colorado Marketplace that we found through a state insurance broker. It looks different for everyone, but it's generally not easy or cheap. Be sure to look into health insurance early in your planning, and budget accordingly.

GROCERIES/ALCOHOL/EATING OUT

Grocery shopping and making your own meals is far cheaper than eating out regularly. It's always cheaper to make your own grub. Then sure, go ahead, crack open a craft beer and reward yourself for a dinner well done (it's cheaper than getting a drink at a bar).

CAMPGROUNDS

Campgrounds can sometimes be unavoidable, depending on your plans for the day. Places like beaches and some national parks are lacking in areas to camp for free. Sites with water and electric hookups will cost more than a tent site.

GYM MEMBERSHIP/SHOWERS

Many van lifers use gym memberships not only for working out but for showers. Look for national and regional fitness chains. Before you join, make sure your membership is good for every location (not just a home gym or a few gyms under the same franchise). Check the map for your gym's locations along your route.

chapter 3 CHOOSING A VEHICLE

Choosing a vehicle is often one of the first steps toward transitioning to a nomadic life-style. Ultimately, finding your home on wheels will come down to a combination of factors including your personal budget, individual preferences, and how you plan to spend your time. Keep in mind that for many folks, the perfect rig might be unattainable at first. It is important to be willing to compromise. Start by writing a list of pros and cons, and decide what you really need to be happy and successful on the road. Since vans tend to be the most popular choice for modern nomads, we will focus this chapter on choosing a van. However, the majority of this information can be used in consideration when purchasing and building out any type of vehicle or trailer.

TYPES OF VANS ON THE MARKET

At a very basic level, there are three types of vans that you will encounter on the road. In order of financial commitment, high to low:

CLASS B MOTORHOMES

A "Class B" motorhome is the smallest of the three classified types of motorhomes. These rigs are given these designations because they are sold and classified as motorhomes. You will be required to register them as Class B and pay for a specific type of insurance. These are usually the most expensive, but they're also built with features that might appeal to those looking for more comforts. Adventure-specific Class B rigs can come fully loaded with 4x4, a lift kit, a hydraulic bed platform, and a fully functioning shower.

PROS

- Fully loaded with features
- Ready for adventure off the lot
- Professional leisure power system
- Usually comes with shore power (ability to connect to AC power supplied at campsites) and water hookups
- Comes with amenities you might not build yourself
- Possible warranty

CONS

- Price
- You'll have to register it as an RV and might pay more for insurance
- Not a stealthy camper van

ALAN & KELLY HARBITTER

ALAN GREW UP IN QUEENS, NEW YORK, and had lived all of his life as a city boy. The Airstreams, though made in Ohio, have more than a bit of New York style. He could see it as his bubble of civilization in the backcountry.

VEHICLE + WHY
2020 16-foot Airstream Bambi—I liked the idea that it provided a self-sufficient mini-home in the middle of nowhere.

TIME ON THE ROAD
Part-time, 6 months

COMFORT ON THE ROAD
I don't think I would have ever explored Lassen Volcanic National Park or Redwood National Park if it involved sleeping on the ground and finding a bathroom in the woods in the middle of the night. The Airstream has opened up a range of adventure options that previously did not exist for me. We live in a country of great natural beauty. I am now able to directly experience so much more of that side of America.

PROFESSIONAL AFTERMARKET CONVERSION

The next option is a van that was purchased new or used and then professionally built out by a van-conversion company. Professional aftermarket conversions won't necessarily be designated Class B because the vehicles are purchased as passenger vehicles. A quality conversion company can deck out a rig just as nicely as something you'd buy off the lot, usually for less money. This option is extremely popular with people who don't have the time to build out a van. Professional van conversions can be expensive, but a skilled shop can do incredible things. Conversion companies are willing to help you design a build that's right for you and that fits a specific budget. Depending on the company, they will either build out a van that you bring to them or sell you a van-conversion package that includes a new built-out van for a single price.

PROS

- Only pay for options that you want
- Professional design and workmanship
- You aren't doing the work, saving your time for other things
- Often professional builds come with warranties
- More stealthy than a professional Class B for sleeping in cities that allow it

CONS

- You have to work with the professional company's timeline, and they are often backed up with work for months
- You may have to compromise on the build-out
- Price

SELF-BUILD

A self-build is a van that was purchased new or used and built out by the owners. This option is known as a DIY, or do it yourself. Building out your own van is the most affordable option and allows you to have an intimate knowledge of your conversion. Honestly, it's also a lot of fun. It's exciting to work with your hands and build something that will bring you endless joy. Converting a van is also time-consuming and can be extremely frustrating. We built a lot of our van, but we did hire a professional to do a few things that we didn't have the skills or tools for. Even if you plan to build out your rig alone, don't be afraid to consult with a professional if you have any questions—especially regarding electricity.

PROS

- Complete freedom on design
- Choice of materials
- Intimate knowledge of your van's inner workings
- Ability to fix the van yourself on the road
- Most affordable

CONS

- Time commitment
- Purchasing and sourcing materials and tools by yourself
- Learning curve

Note: How your vehicle is registered (what type of title you have) is somewhat of a muddy topic. It varies by state, with each state having certain requirements to qualify for an RV title. Each insurance company will have a different policy regarding Class B vs. passenger vehicles. Talk to your insurance provider before you hit the road, and factor extended policy costs into your budget. Keep yourself covered in case of an accident.

CONSIDERATIONS BEFORE PURCHASING

HOW WILL YOU USE THE VAN?

Before you start your build, or when choosing a vehicle that is already built out, take account of what you plan to bring with you and how easily you would like to access those items. Ease of access for often-used items is a huge benefit.

PROTIP

There are multiple van-rental companies in the United States. Find a rental company that rents vans similar to what you're looking for and take it for a spin. Alternatively, you can see if friends will let you stay in their van for a few nights, maybe trade them for a house stay. We spent time in three separate vans before deciding what would best suit our needs.

NEW VS. USED

Whether you choose a new or used vehicle will likely be determined by your budget. A new vehicle will start in great mechanical condition and come with a warranty. If you decide a used vehicle is the right choice, make sure you get it inspected by a licensed mechanic before you purchase it—it will save you money in the long run. When purchasing a used vehicle, there can be hidden maintenance costs. If it's a unique vehicle or from overseas, take into consideration how easy it is to get replacement parts. The vehicle needs to be in good running condition, especially if you plan to take it off-grid. Research if there are any known issues for whatever make and model you are thinking about purchasing. It's also worth looking into recent (or not-so-recent) recalls on the vehicle model you intend to purchase. This goes for both new and used vehicles. Start with "*ProMaster* known issues," "*ProMaster* problems," etc. Insuring a new vehicle often costs more than a used vehicle.

PROTIP

Many previously owned cargo vans are used as work vehicles and have been abused. If you're planning on putting one hundred thousand miles on a used cargo van that already has one hundred thousand miles, there will be many mechanical issues to take care of along the way.

HOW MANY PEOPLE NEED TO FIT IN THE VAN?

Once you purchase your vehicle, adding aftermarket seats is tricky, expensive, and presents safety concerns. Vans come in all shapes and sizes. How many seats you'll need and how many people will need to sleep in the van are numbers you'll want to consider. Do you plan on having friends or significant others travel with you? Will your van be a home for a family?

Car seats can become a huge issue in vans when you try to add aftermarket seating. Car seats should only be placed in forward-facing seats that are bolted to the metal frame of the vehicle. Depending on how many car seats you need, this may greatly affect your build-out plans. We highly recommend getting a certified professional to review your setup for safety and compliance with state and federal car seat regulations.

The number of people that need to sleep in the van will also weigh heavily on your build and potential purchase. A comfortable sleeping setup should be a priority if you plan to live in the van full-time. Taller van lifers may have to build their bed lengthwise (head at the back windows, feet pointing toward the windshield) to make sure they fit.

TO STAND OR NOT TO STAND

If your answer is no, you don't need to stand, then you may want to convert a van with a low roof. This option gives you more choices but could likely end up being a pain in the uhhh . . . back. If you want to be able to stand in your van, you can either purchase a high-roof van or "pop the top" of a low-roof van.

POP-TOP

PROS

- Lower height can be beneficial when driving around town or driving in areas with low-hanging trees
- Some can fit in regular household garages
- Can give you an additional sleeping area if there are more than two people sleeping in your van
- Cooler in the summer and offer more airflow than you can get sleeping in the main cargo area of a hard-sided van

CONS

- Not insulated well and not ideal for four-season travel
- Not as stealthy and secure as hard-sided vans (more obvious someone is sleeping inside)
- Can be broken into more easily
- Fastening solar panels to your pop-top could put extra strain on the struts and cause some mechanical issues
- Potential leaks and other mechanical issues

HIGH ROOF

PROS

- No moving parts
- Less maintenance
- More secure
- Ability to stand
- More stealthy (can disguise as a work vehicle)
- More storage

CONS

- Trouble with covered parking
- Trouble with low-hanging tree branches

PROTIP

If you do opt for a high-roof van, make sure you know the height of your vehicle. This will be helpful in all sorts of situations as you drive through varied terrain and cities.

LOW ROOF

PROS

- Better gas mileage
- Easy to park

CONS

- Less storage
- Can't stand up

GAS MILEAGE + TYPE

If you plan on moving around a lot, the cost of fuel can add up quickly. Research what kind of gas mileage your new vehicle should get and remember that it may be less once you load down your vehicle with the weight of your conversion and everything you need to live. Diesel is an option for many vehicles and has its pros and cons. Besides being able to hang with the truckers, the engine will often last far longer running on diesel and get better gas mileage. Diesel vans often have a higher upfront cost though.

PROTIP

If you're super-handy, eco-friendly, *and* have a diesel engine, you can convert it to run on vegetable oil. This requires a lot of engine know-how and research, but it is super-cool!

FOUR-WHEEL DRIVE VS. TWO-WHEEL DRIVE

The want/need for a four-wheel-drive vehicle is a big talking point in the van life community. People often make their purchase decisions based on that factor alone. Four-by-four can be helpful, but you don't necessarily need it. Our 2x4 front-wheel-drive Ram ProMaster has taken us through the muddy swamps in South Carolina and three years ski bumming in the Rocky Mountains. We don't take our home overlanding (aggressive driving on unmaintained roads), but we do drive on a fair amount of forest service roads and slick surfaces.

If the additional cost of a four-wheel-drive vehicle isn't a deterrent for you, then there really isn't a downside. If you see yourself as more of the overlanding type, it's possible that something like a truck-bed camper or a more capable vehicle is right for you. These vehicles have higher clearance and more robust suspension systems.

FRONT-WHEEL DRIVE VS. REAR-WHEEL DRIVE

We've found that front-wheel drive is superior if you ever plan to drive off the pavement. The traction is much better on most surfaces overall, including in the deep snow. Front-wheel-drive vans tend to be lighter and therefore get better gas mileage and have a higher payload capacity (how much your vehicle can carry). One potential issue with front-wheel drive is that if you overload the rear end of your van, the front wheels could slip on loose terrain when traveling uphill. Another pro for rear wheel drive vans is that they are known to handle corners better than front wheel drive vehicles.

Choosing a vehicle is one of the most important steps to living nomadically, but don't let it stop you in your tracks while planning. Many people outfit the vehicle they already own and set out for a few weeks to see if the lifestyle fits them. Figure out your specific wants and needs, research the options, and get creative!

chapter 4 MAKING YOUR VAN A HOME

ASIDE FROM MAKING THE INITIAL LEAP to a nomadic lifestyle, building out a vehicle could be the most intimidating part of the process. For those who purchase a vehicle, the conversion can end up being the most expensive part. A conversion can be as minimal as a sleeping pad in the back of a Subaru or as decked out as a New York City apartment on wheels.

In this chapter we'll offer some basic conversion guidance along with essential tips and tricks that will help you decide what amenities might be right for you. We'll focus mainly on the basics that are common in most modern adventure rigs.

Much like purchasing a vehicle, the first step in your conversion process should be to build a budget. For the purposes of this chapter, we'll assume that you have already purchased a vehicle and accounted for all associated costs. Think of your conversion as a marathon, not a sprint. If you don't have the money to build your dream van before you hit the road, it's totally fine! Planning a full conversion can be costly and overwhelming. It's okay to start with the basics just to get you out the door and headed for the horizon. Add to your build when time and money allow.

CHRIS STEPHAN

CHRIS WAS A COLORADO WEEKEND WARRIOR always looking for ways to escape his cubical and tiny apartment. He started to notice he was meeting these rad folks whom he looked up to partly because they were living nomadically but mostly because they were pursuing their dreams. He was jealous. Looking back at his life, he found that he always chose the path that felt "safe." Chris decided he couldn't endure "safe" any longer—he needed to pursue his dreams, his hobbies, and most of all he wanted to wake up in beautiful faraway places.

VEHICLE + WHY
2008 Jeep Grand Cherokee—I already owned it and I was crunched for cash.

CONNECT
@tacoplz

TIME ON THE ROAD
Full-time, 10 months

CONVERSION:
I outfitted my eleven-year-old Jeep Grand Cherokee that I already owned with $400 in additions. I cut out the rear seats and installed an under-mattress storage unit. The bed was a full-size memory-foam mattress, I installed a large rooftop box, and mounted a baby-blue motor scooter on the back. I stored my kitchen supplies in a Rubbermaid storage container and brought a cooler for my food supplies. The first week was a little cramped, but I quickly acclimated and grew to love my comfy little setup.

Below are some of the most popular build options (including a few off-the-wall possibilities) and breakdowns including pros, cons, and price considerations. From there you will be able to take this information and apply it to your own budget, needs, and wants.

PROTIP

You may find it helpful to tape off your building plans in the van or physically draw where you plan wires and pipes to go. You can even set up boxes in place of the pieces you plan on building to get a feel for your layout.

NICK WITH FIFTH ELEMENT CAMPING

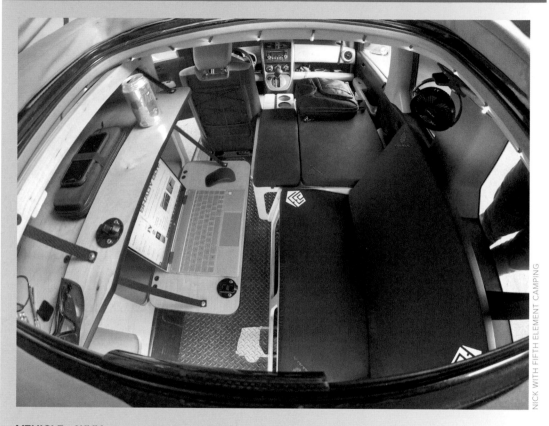

VEHICLE + WHY
Honda Element—it's a reliable, tiny pop-top camper that has a massive interior.

CONNECT
@FifthElementCamping

WORDS OF WISDOM
A build is never truly done. Once you start down this path, you will discover endless new ways to build and design. Have fun with it and don't expect perfection—it's a process and there are joy and lessons in all of it. Scale models and cardboard are extremely helpful. You will find real-world confinements are often more work to draw within than simply cutting and sanding until it fits. Additionally, don't point out flaws in your build to others, you've done great work and mistakes add character, they are not failures. Keep pushing forward. I would find myself stuck with an issue that I thought only another more experienced person could get me out of, but really I just had to sit and think a little longer.

QUIET AND COZY

NOISE REDUCTION

The first item on this list, and likely the first step in your build, is noise reduction. Adding a noise reduction product (like Noico or Fatmat Rattletrap) to the bare inside walls of your vehicle will help make your home a quieter space. If you're camped close to a roadway or next to someone running a generator all night, you'll thank yourself for making the investment. This will also deaden some of the road noise while you're driving. The most popular type of automobile-specific noise reduction comes in peel-and-stick rolls that you can apply directly to the inside walls of your van without any added adhesive. You don't necessarily need to cover the entire interior of your van with the product either. Covering as little as 25 percent of your interior walls will help make your van a quieter place. A fifty-square-foot roll was enough to cover all of the major areas in our Ram ProMaster. To get complete coverage in a large high-roof cargo van, you might need as much as 125 square feet. Expect to spend about $100 on a fifty-square-foot roll. Because this peel-and-stick material will be applied directly to your van's walls, make sure you wipe them down so you have a clean surface to work with.

INSULATION

Insulation regulates internal temperature and can make your van much more comfortable. How well you insulate your van and how much you spend on insulation will depend on climate and travel plans. If the air outside your van is comfortable, little insulation is needed. A ski bum van lifer should opt for heavy insulation.

Just like a down sleeping bag, all insulation is given an R-value. Resistance to heat (R-value) indicates how well a barrier, like insulation, can resist conductive heat. A higher R-value techni-cally means greater insulation power, but keep in mind it is not the only factor. Installation matters a great deal, so don't spend heavily on the material and forget to invest in proper installation. Moisture will inevitably find its way into the van, and proper installation can protect against mold damage.

INSULATION TYPES AND CONSIDERATIONS

3M THINSULATE is generally considered the best option for quality insulation that won't hold moisture or degrade over time. Think of Thinsulate as a puffy jacket for your van. Puffy jackets are filled with the same synthetic material (polyethylene terephthalate). Thin-sulate is very easy to install, doesn't off-gas toxic fumes (release fumes into the air over time), works as an additional sound barrier, and can be easily removed for body repair. Thinsulate actually allows moisture to pass through it, unlike other moisture-resistant insulations, meaning that it won't trap moisture behind it. If you decide Thinsulate is right for you, it's worth investing in some high-quality scissors or shears to help cut the material and speed up the installation process. You can install it simply by cutting pieces to the general size of the area you want to insulate and then using a spray adhesive to attach the Thinsulate to your van. You can glue the Thinsulate directly to the back of your noise reduction material on the inside of your van's walls. It's very malleable so it's easy to slip into those odd-sized nooks and crannies. If you do insulate your van with Thinsulate, you can expect to spend between $300 and $500 depending on how robustly you'd like to insulate your home.

REFLECTIX is an affordable radiant-heat barrier, however, it will only work if it's installed properly. Remember that Reflectix is not insulation, it reflects heat from the sun, preventing it from entering your van. For Reflectix to work at all, there needs to be a minimum of a half-inch gap between the exterior wall of your van and the Reflectix. This allows the Reflectix to reflect the radiant heat that has passed through the wall of your van, preventing it from heating up your home. Don't glue it directly to the wall of your van—that will effectively render the Reflectix useless. It needs to be attached to a separate surface, leaving space between the material and the wall. We have Reflectix glued to the backside of our walls, between the Thinsulate and our wall panels. There is a definite gap, but whether it is helping or not is up for debate. This is where the R-value of a product can be misleading because the R-value of Reflectix varies by the application. You can get fifty square feet of Reflectix with an R-value of 21 for about $25.

SPRAY FOAM comes in industrial kits (often used in houses) or in smaller aerosol cans. Spray foam is on the pricey side as far as insulation goes, and it can be a pain to install. Spray foam can be harmful to inhale, so wear a respirator when installing. We witnessed a full spray-foam job firsthand and it was a messy affair. The thing about spray foam is that it's not meant to be used in a vehicle that twists, shakes, and vibrates. It can begin to degrade behind your walls. We had spray foam in our first van, and after a couple of years, it turned mostly to dust. That dust became airborne when we drove, and it ended up causing us some respiratory issues. You can use the smaller aerosol spray foam cans to fill in odd gaps, but we don't recommend it for your entire van. Spray foam is also known to off-gas harmful chemicals. However, spray foam does work well for sound reduction.

You've most likely seen **FOAM BOARD INSULATION** before. It's used on houses and other construction projects. Foam board insulation comes in two main types: polyisocyanurate (Polyiso) foam board and extruded polystyrene (XPS) foam board. Of the two, Polyiso is a more environmentally friendly choice. It's fairly inexpensive, won't absorb moisture, and is easy enough to work with. It also has the highest R-value (R-6.5 to R-6.8) of any rigid insulation. If installed properly, it can act as a radiant-heat barrier as well. The kicker here is that Polyiso must be installed correctly to work. If you're not careful, you can create air pockets behind the insulation that can trap moisture. XPS (R-5.0) works similarly, but the manufacturing process calls for the use of hydrofluorocarbons. XPS is also known to off-gas. Both options work well as insulation under your floor because they can handle being compressed without compromising the insulation properties.

Other Options

There are some neat eco-friendly and recycled insulation products on the market, most notably recycled denim and wool. Recycled denim offers a great R-value, but its tendency to absorb moisture should rule it out for most van lifers. Think about the last time you spilled something on your jeans—how quickly did that dry? Sheep's wool is another interesting option. Similar to merino wool base layers, sheep's wool insulation offers great moisture-management properties at an affordable price. It also acts as a natural air filter.

Fifty square feet of denim insulation, R-value 19, costs around $50.

Fifty square feet of wool insulation, R-value 19, costs around $140.

ALL THINGS ELECTRIC

Auxiliary power, or leisure power, means different things to different people. No doubt you'll want some extra power when you're out on your great adventure, but how much power will you actually need? This will influence many of your build decisions down the road. Will you only be charging a cellphone? Do you plan on running a refrigerator? There are plenty of low-cost options that can provide a rechargeable power source.

We run a refrigerator, instant pot, and a coffee grinder. We also work full-time from our van so we need enough power to keep our computers and all of our camera gear up

and running. We opted to power everything with solar rather than incorporating propane or using a generator. Keep in mind an improperly wired electrical system can be a serious fire hazard.

Even if you plan on having a professional install your electric system, as we found out the hard way, it's important to have a basic understanding of how your power system works. The reality of van life is that things break or stop working fairly often. If you spend a lot of time cruising down forest service roads that are so rutted out that you'll have to put down your copy of *The Falcon Guide to Van Life*, then connections will inevitably shake loose. Being able to make some simple on-the-fly fixes and repairs will make your traveling days a lot less stressful.

Aside from where all of those wires are connected, you'll also want to have a solid understanding of how much power you are generating and how much power you are using. How are you going to charge your batteries? We traveled for a full year only charging our auxiliary batteries with our alternator. If you skip the solar panels, make sure you never drain your batteries too low. Battery health is extremely important for maintaining a solid power system.

NIK & ALLISON WHITE

ALLISON HAD JUST FINISHED GRADUATE SCHOOL and was ready for a sabbatical, and Nik was working remotely already, so suddenly they didn't have work or school requiring them to stay in one place. They made a list of dream options, and full-time RV life seemed like the best and most fun future.

VEHICLE + WHY
1989 Winnebago—it was a Craigslist special!

CONNECT
www.therecklesschoice.com

TIME ON THE ROAD
Full-time, 2 years

GOING SOLAR

A lot of our solar planning was done based on what we could find for cheap on Craigslist. We did a basic analysis of how much power we would need to run our laptops, microwave, lights, and water pump and then gave ourselves a lot of leeway—but we didn't really do an exacting analysis in any way. We probably used about 500 to 1,000-watt-hours of electricity per day including running all of our laptops, using an electric microwave, and sometimes running our refrigerator on the electric system.

We had four 265-watt solar panels that fed four large AGM lead-acid batteries. We also had a 3,000-watt hybrid inverter/charger from Victron that was awesome. The hybrid inverter charger allowed us to do some really cool things like replace our generator with a very small one and never need to use a 30-amp power cable. We also could plug into normal electrical outlets and not worry about tripping a breaker.

LEISURE POWER

Some people have no problem traveling with a stand-alone rechargeable battery pack. There are many brands on the market and some have the ability to hold enough charge to keep your laptop and phone energized for several days. These can usually be purchased with solar panels and charged simply by letting the panels sit in the sun for a day. They can also charge while plugged into the wall at a cafe while you slowly sip a cup of coffee and catch up on some work.

Most modern nomads want a power system more like what you will find in an RV. This means being able to power most 12-volt appliances with enough juice left over to run your vent fan, power internal lighting, and keep your cell phone at 100 percent.

If you want an auxiliary power system (also known as leisure power in RVs), start with a battery bank. Essentially, you'll have an extra set of batteries that will charge off of your vehicle's alternator while you're driving. If you include solar, you'll have two different options for charging. Plan and design your electrical system before you purchase anything that will require a power source. If you have a professional install your electric system, consult with them on your power needs first.

There are two types of electrical current: direct current (DC) and alternating current (AC). Anything that you would plug into a cigarette lighter, such as handheld electronics or anything with a USB cable, is run off of DC power. Leisure batteries (the secondary power bank) found in camper vans also run off of DC power. AC power is typically what you find in a modern home. Anything with a three-prong connector will need AC power to work. Most camper vans' leisure power systems are based around 12v DC power.

When designing your power system, first figure out how much power you'll actually need. Add up the total number of amps that all of your appliances will use. Some appliances will list the amps used in the owner's manual and some will be listed in watts. If only watts are listed, divide the watts by volts (12). In the case of a standard leisure power system, volts will always equal 12 due to the 12v DC battery bank. For example, if you are running a 90-watt appliance, and you want to determine how many amps that appliance is going to use, then divide 90 (watts) by 12 (volts) to get 7.5 (amps). Once you know the number of amps that each appliance uses, take a guess at how many hours each day you will use that appliance. Multiply the number of amps needed for each appliance by the number of hours you need them to be powered. If that 7.5-amp appliance will be used for two hours, that will require 15 amp-hours of power. This will give you a total number of amp-hours (AH) needed for each appliance. Add all of the amps hours needed together, building in a little extra. Say, in total, you found that you need 100AH of power each day. That means your battery bank will need to be at least 100AH.

How much power a battery can hold is measured in amp hours (or AH). The higher the AH rating, the higher the charge your battery can hold. You can figure out how long your batteries will last by knowing the AH rating of your battery bank. If you have one 25AH battery, and you are running a fan that is pulling 1AH from your battery bank, your battery will be dead in 25 hours.

Helpful Equations

Watts = amps x volts
Amps = watts/volts
AH = amps x hours

BATTERY TYPES

Flooded Lead Acid Batteries

These are the cheapest option, but they need some routine maintenance to help them function properly. You'll need to periodically add water to the batteries. The chemical reaction that happens inside these batteries causes them to emit harmful gases, so they need to be kept in a vented external compartment that is sealed off from the main cabin. For this reason, they're not the best choice of leisure batteries for most rigs.

Gel Batteries

Gel batteries are a type of sealed lead-acid battery. They function in a similar manner to their flooded counterpart but they are sealed. This means they are safer to use indoors and theoretically won't off-gas. However, they still need some maintenance, they hold a smaller amount of energy in relation to their size, and they need to be charged at a slower rate than some of the other options. For these reasons, we also recommend against gel batteries.

AGM Batteries

AGM (absorbed glass mat) batteries are another type of sealed lead-acid battery. They are the most popular choice for many modern nomads. They can charge much faster than the options listed above. In some cases, they can be charged up to five times faster than flooded batteries. AGM batteries also have the ability to "deep cycle." This means you can drain the batteries down further without actually damaging the battery itself. They also don't require any maintenance and don't need to be vented. Perhaps the best thing about AGM batteries is that they work at and can be charged in the widest range of temperatures. We needed a battery bank that could withstand being in the extreme cold, so for our conversion, we chose to use AGM batteries.

Lithium-Ion Batteries

Lithium-ion batteries have the highest upfront cost of all the popular leisure battery types. However, they have a life cycle of up to ten years so they may end up being the cheapest option in the long run. Lithium-ion batteries can also be drained almost entirely without causing any permanent damage to the batteries. This type of battery has zero off-gassing. The real drawback of these batteries is that they cannot be charged at low temperatures. If you will be traveling in colder weather (at or near freezing), you might want to rule out lithium-ion batteries.

CHARGING YOUR BATTERIES

Once you've chosen a battery type, decide how you want to charge them. You have three options and you can do any combination of the three or all of them. The first option is to have the alternator in your vehicle charge your battery bank via split charging. This means that the alternator is charging both your starter battery and your leisure batteries. You'll want to make sure that your starter battery is isolated so you don't draw power from it over to your leisure battery.

The next option is to add solar. If you would like to harness the sun (and most modern nomads do), add solar panels to your set up. These can be attached to the roof, or detached so you can position them once you find camp. Solar is also great for keeping your batteries topped off and in tiptop shape (a charged battery is a happy battery). If you want to add solar, you'll need at least one solar panel and a charge controller. The panel captures the sun and sends the energy to your charge controller that in turn sends regulated and usable energy to your battery bank.

The final option, and something you see on most RVs and Class B rigs, is shore power. Shore power is just another term for being able to plug your rig's electrical system into a standard 110v outlet. The term comes from the power source boats use when docked onshore. The concept is the same for RVs and vans as it is with boats. Shore power will charge your battery bank and has the ability to power your van's full electrical system. Shore power is helpful if you are in an area without much sun and you can't/don't want to run the engine to charge your batteries. Shore power is also a good way to be able to use appliances like an air conditioner that require high amounts of energy.

Power Inverters

In a standard Class B camper van, as mentioned above, the leisure power system generates 12-volt DC power. That's why most of the appliances you see in adventure rigs and RVs are specifically 12v appliances and are a bit different than what you would use at home. However, if you have a need for 120v AC power like you see in a house, then you should add an inverter into the mix. A power inverter converts the 12v DC power that's drawn from your leisure batteries into 120v AC power. Any appliance that you would normally plug into a three-prong outlet will need to be plugged into your power inverter to work. There are several types of power inverters but most nomads prefer a pure sine power inverter. This type of inverter will most accurately reproduce power like you have at home. There is plenty of math that goes into figuring out how large an inverter you need. Without going too far into it, we'll say that a 2,000-watt pure sine inverter should be enough to power anything you want as long as your batteries can handle it.

Power Charger/Inverter

If you plan to add shore power to your rig and you also want to install an inverter, save yourself some trouble and install a charger/inverter. This two-in-one piece of equipment not only allows you to bring shore power into the mix, it will also be your power inverter. You could install both a power inverter and a battery charger converter, but it would require more wiring, more money, and more space.

There's much more to your electrical system than what we've covered in this section. You'll need some additional pieces of gear like the proper gauge wire and a fuse box among other things. Electrical systems can be dangerous if not properly installed and maintained. You can purchase custom wiring diagrams that will help you make sure everything is wired in the proper manner. As you research the individual types of gear listed above, it's important to purchase the appropriate equipment for the size and type of battery bank that you chose to install. Before you start gathering materials, it would be wise to consult with a professional. Something as simple as an improperly wired power inverter can easily start an electrical fire in your new home.

CLIMATE CONTROL

VENTS AND VENT FANS

Air circulation is the key to proper moisture management and temperature regulation in your van. Simple 12v ceiling vents from brands like Dometic and MaxxAir are an affordable solution that you'll find in the majority of camper vans out on the road. You can find these vents at all different price points with all types of fancy features.

A nonmotorized ceiling vent (essentially just a hole in your roof that allows hot air and moisture to escape but doesn't allow rain to get in) is the most basic option. These vents are easy on the budget, but they don't work very well. We had a nonmotorized vent in our

---

PROTIP

We purchased a $22 USB-powered desk fan and hung it above our heads to use while we're sleeping. It helps keep us cool on hot summer nights when our vent fan just doesn't cut it. We also like how it circulates air in the back of our van. We use a DC 5-volt nine-inch fan and it works wonders. We've run ours for over two thousand hours and it still works flawlessly, though we have had to clean it multiple times because it gets so much use.

first van and we found it to be woefully inadequate for removing hot air *or* reducing moisture. Consider a vent with a fan that can actually circulate air in or out.

The van-life standard is a multispeed roof vent that can suck moisture and warm air out of the van—it's magical. If you want to get fancy with it, there are vents that have automatic temperature controls, remote control access, and vents that will close automatically if they sense rain. When balancing our budget we decided that all we really cared about was getting a fan that would move air and keep out the rain, so we decided on a simple base model Fantastic Fan, and it works great! If we had to do it again, we would get a model that could reverse and blow in fresh air from outside also rather than just suck the air out. Keep in mind that while having conveniences like a vent that will automatically open and close can be nice, it also presents more opportunities for things to break while you're out in the backcountry. We like to keep it simple.

If you only decide to put in one roof vent, consider putting the vent over your bed. This will draw fresh air in (usually from a cracked window near the front or middle of the van) and circulate it throughout to keep you cool while you're sleeping. Another good option is to have a ceiling vent over your kitchen area. Placing your vent above your kitchen will help you suck out any smoke and carbon monoxide that is created while you are cooking. Before you cut a hole in the roof of your van to install a fan, it's important to consider whether or not you will have solar panels on your roof or any type of roof rack system.

AWNINGS

You've probably seen them on adventure vans at the gear shop and at the trailhead. An awning can be a great asset depending on what type of travel you plan on doing. We went for two years without an awning in our van. However, looking back on all of the time we spent repositioning our van so we could block the powerful western sun just for an

PROTIP

The major bonus of having an awning in rainy weather is that you can expand your livable space. If you're traveling and hit a bad weather window, you'll find yourself spending a lot of time cooped up inside your van. Being able to add outdoor space and still keep dry can raise spirits.

hour's worth of shade, we should have thought of a solution sooner. Just like vent fans, awnings can come with a host of fancy features like a wind sensor and remote controls, but you definitely pay for the extras. High winds are a real concern with awnings because many companies won't warranty their products if they have wind damage. However, if you do a lot of camping in sunny areas, it's really nice to be able to create your own shade. It opens up your campsite options if you don't need to rely on finding a spot with trees. We weren't quite ready to make the financial leap for an electric/automatic awning so we purchased a foldable awning. We use a less expensive awning that you have to put up yourself and secure to the top of your vehicle with suction cups. It works well in high winds, and if it breaks, you're not out $2,000. It does take a few minutes to set up so we only use it if we're going to camp in the same spot for a few days.

AIR-CONDITIONING

While it is possible to run an RV-style air-conditioning unit in a van, it requires some forethought and financial commitment. If you plan to spend long days in the hot desert or warm and humid nights by the ocean, then having an air-conditioning unit might be the right choice. Companies like Dometic have been making great quality air conditioners for RVs and big rigs for a long time. However, before you lay down the cash, you'll need to decide how you are going to power the unit. It is possible to run air-conditioning on an off-grid solar setup, but you'll need a huge bank of lithium batteries. We would only recommend installing an air-conditioning unit if you will be traveling with a generator that you are willing to fire up every time you want some cool air or plan to set up your van with shore power hookups. Of course, if you go with shore power, you'll only be able to run your air-conditioning when you have a place to plug in your van. Shore power works as a viable option if your plans include staying in campgrounds or near electrical outlets the majority of the time.

WINDOW SHADES

One of the best ways to keep the heat out, and your privacy safe, is window covers. There are a few options, ranging from fabric hung with magnets to custom-made window shades for specific vehicle models. We have a combination of both in our ProMaster. We sewed curtains to fit the back windows and attached them with Velcro. This is also where we proudly display our pin collection. We purchased custom-fit window shades for the front, instead of using a curtain, so we could continue to use that space when we wanted privacy. Window shades also help keep the heat out of your van.

HEATERS

Many nomads travel full-time without a heater in their van. If you plan to travel in the mountains or in cold weather, having a heater is a great option. You may think "I'll just bundle up and use a lot of blankets." We tried that, and it was tolerable for a while, but waking up on a frosty morning to make coffee is a lot more enjoyable when your van isn't below freezing on the inside. If you are traveling full-time in the winter, you will likely spend a lot more time in your van than you would in the summer due to poor weather and lack of daylight hours. Having a heater is also a good way to keep your liquids from freezing overnight. We love our heater. Just hearing it run offers a familiar sense of comfort in our cozy home.

PROTIP

If you plan to run any type of heater in your van, you should install a combination carbon monoxide and explosive gas detector and make sure you have a fire extinguisher onboard. We recommend both of these as essential safety equipment, but carbon monoxide poisoning is no joke and this information is worth repeating.

GASOLINE AND DIESEL FORCED-AIR FURNACES

Gasoline and diesel forced-air furnaces are a solid option for heating your van. This is especially true if you don't plan on outfitting your rig with propane. These heaters can be expensive, but they are also some of the safest and most reliable vehicle heaters on the market. Long-haul truckers have been using the diesel version of these heaters to keep the inside of their cabs warm for a long time. These heaters can be somewhat complicated to install. The two big names in forced-air furnaces are Webasto and Eberspächer. There is a world of off-brand forced-air furnaces available online that some will swear by. The knockoffs may not come with the same quality and warranties that you'll find with the name brands. Both of these high-end heaters draw directly from your van's fuel tank, eliminating the need for an additional fuel source. They are extremely fuel efficient. We've run our Webasto for twelve consecutive hours many times and barely noticed a difference in our fuel gauge. The heaters are set up so they can't drain your fuel tank completely—so you'll never have to worry about running

out of gas while you're sleeping and the heater is chugging away. Another big plus is the external exhaust. You won't have to be concerned about carbon monoxide or other harmful fumes inside your vehicle. Forced-air furnaces produce a dry heat so you won't be introducing additional moisture into your van. These heaters also require very little maintenance after they are installed. If you're spending time above five-thousand feet, purchase a unit with a high altitude adjustment.

PROTIP

The gasoline-burning furnaces are known to suffer from carbon buildup inside the unit, air intake, and exhaust pipes. This will only be a problem with heavy usage, but you can do some easy preventative maintenance to help combat this. Every once in a while, disconnect the exhaust pipe on the underside of your vehicle. Take an air compressor (like you would fill your tires with at the gas station) and blow compressed air through the exhaust pipe to clear it of any carbon buildup. If you do this we recommend wearing eye protection and a face covering/respirator.

WOODBURNING STOVE

A woodburning stove is an Instagram-worthy addition to any camper van. Fuel is cheap (or free), the heat is dry, and your van will feel like a cozy cabin on wheels. However, there are some drawbacks to having a woodburning stove in your vehicle. The first is that burning wood puts off carbon monoxide, so once again, you must ensure proper ventilation of the van at all times. This means having fresh air circulating throughout the van via a cracked window and your vent fan.

These stoves are manually operated and maintained so you'll have to make sure to always have wood on hand and the energy to feed the fire. They also require an elaborate installation process to ensure they are venting properly and are not a fire hazard. Wood-stoves do require some ongoing maintenance to keep them in working order. They will need to be cleaned from time to time, you will need to cut your wood to an appropriate size (but this, too, could create some Instagram-worthy moments), and you may need to feed the fire several times during the night. You will also need to make room in your van for a woodburning stove. Even the smallest woodstoves take up more room on the interior than most of the alternatives.

12-VOLT ELECTRIC HEATER

Small electric heaters can be a viable heating option and don't need to be built in to your camper van. They put off a consistent dry heat and require little to no installation. They are also fairly affordable. However, anything with a heating element will draw a large amount of power from your battery bank. You may only want to consider a 12v electric heater if you have a large battery bank or plan to be connected to shore power for the majority of the time.

EXTERNALLY VENTED PROPANE HEATER

Propane has been a go-to heating source for RVs for a long time and it's still widely popular today. These RV-style heaters generally require an external propane tank as a source of fuel. You won't be able to get by with the little green disposable canisters that you might use for a two-burner stove. If you plan to outfit your van with propane for cooking and hot water, then an externally vented propane heater (like a Propex) is a good heating option. An externally vented Propex-style heater shouldn't bring moisture into your vehicle like other propane heaters. These heaters are generally considered safe and won't introduce dangerous fumes into your rig.

STAND-ALONE PROPANE HEATER

Stand-alone propane heaters are the most budget-friendly option. They also provide heat quickly and efficiently. For this reason, they are probably the most common heating source for folks with DIY conversions. However, saving a few dollars can come at a bigger price. Stand-alone propane heaters, like Mr. Heater Buddy heaters, come with risks when using them indoors. The online van life communities will debate this until the end of time. At the end of the day, you have to be comfortable with the level of risk that you are taking when burning fuels inside your home on wheels. The official instructions that come with the Mr. Heater Buddy heaters state that they are safe to use indoors. They do not specifically say they are safe to use inside a vehicle while you are sleeping. They do come with an oxygen sensor that will theoretically shut the heater off if oxygen gets too low. This, in turn, should protect you from carbon monoxide poisoning caused by a lack of oxygen. If you decide to use one of these heaters, you must ensure proper ventilation and utilize a carbon monoxide and explosive gas detector. We don't like the idea of fuel combustion inside our van while we're sleeping—it's just too risky for us. We do all we can to keep carbon monoxide outside our van and keep the hallucinating to a minimum. It's important to note that this style of heater will also introduce moisture inside your vehicle. Moisture is the enemy and can lead to mold problems inside your home. We would urge you to consider a safer method of heating than using this style of propane heater. That being said, many people do use them and swear by them.

WHERE THERE'S WATER THERE'S A WAY

FRESH WATER

If you hit the road with only one thing, it would be wise to choose fresh water. There are many different ways to handle your freshwater needs. If you are traveling long-term, having a working sink and running water has a lot of benefits and comes with a relatively small price tag. On the most basic level, this requires two water tanks. One water tank to hold your fresh water and the second tank to hold the "gray," or dirty, water that you need to capture until you can find a proper place to dispose of it. From there you'll need a way to move water out of your freshwater tank to a place that you can use it, and a way to capture your dirty water and move it to your gray-water tank. This is how your sink at home functions. You might be thinking, "couldn't I just drain my sink straight outside onto the ground? It would only be food scraps from my dishes, and I only use biodegradable soaps." The answer is yes, you could, but you shouldn't! Always leave no trace. Letting your gray water drain out of the bottom of your van can attract wildlife, impact the environment, and start to smell. It doesn't really matter what type of setup you have, find a way to

catch your gray water and hold on to it until you can dump it somewhere legal and safe. When thinking about how you want to deal with water, you have a few options.

SIMPLE HAND-PUMP SINKS

A sink and faucet system that works similarly to your sink at home is surprisingly easy to build and affordable. You can find several options for hand pump faucets online. The faucet will usually be a combination of a faucet and a pump. With this setup, rather than being able to just turn on the tap and have free-flowing water, you have to manually pump the water from your tank to your faucet. Some

---

PROTIP

We recommend avoiding plastic hand-pump faucets. In our experience, while they do work, the plastic pieces don't hold up to everyday use and they will eventually start to leak.

---

options on the market have a hand pump right next to the faucet. This can be tricky when trying to do dishes or wash your hands. One hand will always need to be pumping water. Other options on the market use a foot pump instead of a hand pump. A plus to a manual pump is that you will use less water than if you had an electric pump. The downside is that they can be a pain for everyday life.

FULL ELECTRIC-PUMP SINK

For this setup to work in your vehicle, you will need a leisure electrical system. The pros of having this setup are obvious. It's the most like home and the most convenient. In our experience it also requires less maintenance than manual-pump-style sinks. The downsides are that you use more water and you'll have to wire a pump to your electrical system—and you'll probably still battle over who has to do dishes after dinner. You will also have to purchase an electric pump that will add roughly $100 to the cost of your sink.

PROTIP

Install an accumulator tank between the pump and faucet. An accumulator tank does exactly what its name says it does: It accumulates water and pressure inside of it and in turn, it delivers a more consistent flow of water to your faucet. The accumulator tank will also, theoretically, extend the life of your pump.

PROTIP

Install a "kill switch" for your electric pump. Wire the switch between your pump and your auxiliary fuse box. Sometimes our pump would kick on in the middle of the night, even if we weren't using the faucet. Our pump was below our bed and having the ability to turn off the power to it so it doesn't run while we're sleeping has been a nice bonus.

SHOWERS

This is a tricky topic because logistically, building a shower into a vehicle doesn't make a lot of sense. They require a lot of maintenance, they introduce moisture into your home, they take up valuable space, and they can be expensive to build. We have traveled for several years without an official shower and while we may have had a few days unfit for public appearances, it's been mostly a great choice for us. However, if you're not into roughing it, it is possible to build a shower into your van. If you decide to go this route, you'll obviously need to build in quite a lot of infrastructure to make this work. You might just find it to be more trouble than it's worth. Below are some alternative shower setups for the modern nomad.

Solar Shower

You may have seen the inexpensive solar showers that you can hang from a tree. These work well for a weekend trip, but they really aren't built with the quality that you need for the long haul. These also require you to be able to hang the bag from a tree or your van. We popped two in two weeks. It was so much fun!

There are also many interesting options that can be mounted to a vehicle's roof rack. The Road Shower from Yakima can hold ten gallons of fresh water, mounts to your roof rack, and is heated by the sun. Refilling roof-mounted showers can be somewhat challenging when you are traveling because you need to find a hose or remove the shower from your roof. The upside is that since they are already on your roof, you never have to remember to set it out in the sun to warm it up, and the pressure is created by gravity.

Pressure Shower

This is the option we settled on. While our pressure shower is also a solar shower, it comes with a few extra bells and whistles that make it more convenient than the budget solar shower option listed above. NEMO makes an excellent foot pump pressure shower that, when left in the sun, will warm up and deliver a surprisingly refreshing "shower." We say "shower" because you're never going to get the full shower feeling. It's still basically spraying down with water, washing with soap, then spraying down again. It works to keep grime out of your sheets but not to look presentable for a first date. Our pressure shower holds seven gallons of water and we can squeeze out between six and eight "showers" for both of us before we need to refill it.

You can create a little privacy room for yourself by using the two backdoors of your van and a tarp. It actually works quite well for privacy and fending off the wind if you accidentally wait until the sun goes down to wash off. While using the sun is a great way to warm your water, we've found that at least half the time our showers end up being cold. We are very used to cold showers.

CAMP TOILETS

There are definitely some pros to having an onboard toilet. They're good for folks who will be spending time camping in urban areas or for people with health issues that require easy access to a bathroom. There is also the comfort factor. If you have issues with pit toilets or public restrooms, being able to go in the comfort of your van might be something that you really value. There are places that you can't camp without a way to pack out your waste. It also might just make you feel more at home with a travel throne.

There are also sizable downsides to having a toilet onboard that led us to choose not to build a toilet into our van. First off, space was at a premium for us. We weighed the pros and cons, and in our current situation, we decided we valued the space more than we valued having a toilet. Also, traveling as a couple, we decided that it would make for some awkward mornings if one of us had to use the bathroom while the other was making breakfast. The other thing that led us to ditch the toilet was the fact that at some point, you're going to have to empty them. Depending on the extent of your conversion, you might have a black-water holding tank, making the emptying process much easier. Black-water tanks are common in RVs, and they have to be emptied regularly. However, most of the common toilets found in adventure vans have self-contained holding tanks that have to be emptied every few days, and you'll need to find a safe, sanitary, and legal place to dump your waste like an actual toilet or an RV dump station. It's smelly and it can be messy. Depending on the type of toilet, it might have an external exhaust fan, but you'll still get a whiff every now and then. Many portable toilets also require the use of chemicals, and we didn't want a chemical smell in our van either. Here are some of the most common types of toilets that we see out in the wild.

Collapsible Toilets

One of the easiest and most budget-friendly options is to use a portable and collapsible toilet seat in conjunction with a GO Anywhere Toilet Kit Waste Bag that can be purchased online or at many outdoors retailers. The most popular one on the market is the Cleanwaste GO Anywhere Portable Toilet Seat. The setup is fairly straightforward—it comes with a collapsible seat that can be stashed away until you need it. To use it, you simply set up the seat, attach the bag, and do your business into the bag. Glamorous, right? The kit includes Poo Powder to cut down on odor, and it turns your waste into a gel that is safe for disposal. It's not glamorous, but it has the endorsement of the Bureau of Land Management and the Leave No Trace Program in conjunction with the US Forest Service. The bags are landfill-approved and can be disposed of in a regular trash can. The downside is that the bags are expensive and the cost will add up over time. You'll also need to set it up before each use. There are less expensive options that function in a similar manner. They are essentially just a bucket with a toilet seat on top.

Cassette Toilets

Looking for something a little more permanent to make your buns feel at home? A cassette toilet or cartridge toilet is a permanent toilet with a portable holding tank or black-water tank. This style of toilet is widely used in European camper vans and motorhomes and you can even find them in many Class B rigs in the United States. The Thetford Cassette Toilet is one of the most popular options on the market. These toilets tend to resemble a toilet similar to what you have at home. They are sealed and, theoretically, shouldn't smell, although we've heard some anecdotes that report the opposite. These toilets do require chemicals as well as freshwater and electric hookups so the installation process is something to be aware of beforehand. The black-water tank is only removable from the exterior of the vehicle so you'll need to cut a hole and install an access door (sold separately) to complete your installation. These toilets are fixed in place above a permanent and dedicated black-water tank, and once installed, you won't be able to move them. You'll need to dump the black-water tank into a regular toilet or find another way to dump it properly. This can be unsavory for some. These also have the potential to freeze in the wintertime. There's an image for you!

Portable Toilets

As far as van life goes, this is the most common option that we see people adding to their conversions. These toilets have the look and feel of a cassette toilet but can be purchased at a fraction of the cost. They are (just as the name suggests) portable, so they won't be permanently fixed inside your vehicle. They still take up space, but being able to move them around is a nice option. People sometimes build these onto drawers or sliders so they can easily stash them when they're not in use. Portable toilets don't require a freshwater hookup or electricity to use. They use a freshwater holding tank that you can fill and a hand pump to flush the waste into the removable black-water tank underneath the bowl. These toilets also require chemicals and have the potential to freeze in cold weather.

Composting Toilets

Composting toilets are a compelling toilet option for your conversion. They are also the most expensive option. These eco-friendly toilets don't use water or chemicals and are generally less odorous and easier to empty. The defining feature of a composting toilet is that it separates the liquids from the solids. When you flush, the solids go into one tank and the liquids go into a second tank. This helps prevent odor but also allows the liquid to evaporate from the solids tank (with the help of an externally routed fan) and allows it to eventually turn to compost. The solids tank uses a bulking material such as peat moss or coconut coir to help dry out and break down the solid waste. If left for a long enough time, you can actually use your solid waste as fertilizer. While doing this during long-term travel isn't very feasible, it is a possibility. You can also throw the solid waste in a normal trash can while emptying the liquid waste into a normal toilet. This option will need a small power source to run the fan. It also has to be built into your rig—so once it's installed you won't be able to move it.

chapter 5 LESS *IS* MORE

DOWNSIZING WAS THE STEP OF VAN LIFE PREPARATION when we felt our lives were truly about to change. The paring down of our material things was a long and arduous process. We packed what we thought we needed, then, of course, after a few months in the van, we found we had packed way too much and pared down even more.

Lucky for soon-to-be van lifers, it is trendy to be minimalistic. There are thirty-day minimalist challenges, 42.2 million returns on Google for "capsule wardrobe," and Marie Kondo is a household name. You can even watch the documentary *Minimalism: A Documentary About the Important Things* to get a head start on figuring out what's important. Start by taking a look at some minimalist resources to get you in the right mindset.

Having less clutter is relaxing, and no one knows that more intimately than those living in their vehicles. Trade having too much stuff for freedom—it's worth it one thousand times over.

No matter how you choose to pare down your belongings, start now. Start today, after you finish reading this chapter. Don't wait until the last minute and end up throwing away things that could have been sold or donated. Your future self will thank you!

WHAT TO DO WITH YOUR BELONGINGS THAT YOU CAN'T TAKE WITH YOU: There are packing lists in chapter 14. Start there to get an idea of what you might need (or *not* need!) to begin your journey. These items range from the essential to more indulgent nice-to-have items. After you take a look at those lists, take stock of what else you own, which is probably plenty of miscellaneous life items that are now unnecessary. Where do these items go?

KEEP, SELL, DONATE, TOSS

Start by putting everything in one place. It will be easier to compare, keep, donate, sell, and toss items when you can see everything you need to deal with. If that isn't possible, go from room to room creating piles, and then combine them at the end.

KEEP

This pile will contain items that are irreplaceable. Everything you keep holds weight in some way, so place items in this category carefully. These items could include:

- Expensive personal gear you can't fit in your vehicle
- Artwork you don't want to sell or donate
- Clothing for a different season that won't fit in your van storage
- Expensive electronics you don't want to repurchase when you're living in a stationary situation
- Expensive furniture if you have any
- Anything that holds a sentimental value that you want to keep safe

There are a few options for where to keep your "keep" items. We recommend buying a few big plastic bins and labeling them with detailed notes on the outside. Permanent marker and duct tape work well for this process. If everything is well labeled, when you need to retrieve something, it will be easy to find. Pests can't get in, and the dust stays out. Bins are also easy to move if something happens at the space where you are keeping these items. You may leave them with a friend or family member if someone has extra space and a kind heart. Or you can get a small storage unit. The storage unit is great for furniture if you have plenty of that, but not great because it adds to your monthly operation fees.

SELL

This should be a big pile! While expenses drop significantly when you move into a van, it can still be a tight financial situation if you don't have a full-time remote/traveling job. There are many options for where to sell your extra items, depending on what you're trying to get rid of.

Gear shops have used gear programs and there are a multitude of options online. Selling items can become a full-time job. We had excel spreadsheets and a mini-shipping center set up. Here are some examples of ways to sell:

- REI garage parking lot sale
- eBay
- Craigslist
- Facebook Marketplace
- Local Facebook groups
- Friends and family
- Yard sale

DONATE

This pile is for items you don't want to store or sell. Clothing is one of the hardest things to pare down. Our best recommendation is to keep three seasons worth of clothing in your van and summer or winter clothing in a plastic bin with what you're storing. Then switch out your seasonal clothing as you need it. The big puffy jackets didn't seem right in ninety-degree weather, and the tank tops are annoying when it's below zero degrees. This isn't possible if you don't plan on returning home after you leave. In that case, grab a few essentials for each season and layers. Here are some options of where to start with your donation pile:

- Goodwill
- Domestic violence shelters
- Homeless shelters
- Local gear shops
- Local children's groups (think Girl Scouts or Big City Mountaineers)
- The Arc
- The Salvation Army

There are also item-specific donation groups. Old fancy dresses can go to Project G.L.A.M., and used but not destroyed running shoes can find their way to Soles4Souls. Everything has a place, just like in a van. So take the time to find the right donation location for you and your gently used items. The landfill, and those receiving your donated items, will thank you.

TOSS/RECYCLE

There will be some amount of items you can't keep, sell, or donate. These items should be properly disposed of. A lot of our motivation to move into a van was to create a smaller footprint. Throwing away these things felt contrary to our end goal, but it was a necessary step to get there.

PROTIP

There are bins located in the entryways to most Best Buy stores that allow you to recycle different types of electronics and unneeded cables.

NOT SURE

How did another category sneak in here? The "Not Sure" category might be your biggest pile of them all. Making decisions about your items is hard, and often one item will fit in multiple categories. You could sell it, but it'll be a hassle, you could donate it, but you don't know where. Create a Not Sure pile, and save it for last. Once you've dealt with everything else, hopefully you will have a better idea about how to approach these items.

HOW TO TRAVEL LIGHTLY

Simply by spending a few nights in your van, you will find out what is useful, and what is just taking up space. Categories we struggled with included clothing (we needed far less than expected), kitchen items (we used and washed our favorites over and over), and entertainment items (we needed more than we started out with). Don't underestimate the amount of downtime you will have if you're not working a full-time remote job. Even if you are, there will be many weeknights where you are parked with no service and nothing to do. There's only so much "stare at beautiful scenery" you can do each evening. Add in a few entertainment items like cards, crafts, letters to send friends, books (we both have e-readers and a library subscription, which have proved invaluable), or a favorite downloaded TV show.

Your wants and needs change dramatically, and suddenly what you used to use daily becomes useless. Our best advice is to take a four- or five-day trip (or a long weekend, depending on your van plans), but stay close to a home base. This way you will get an idea of what you need and what you want.

MAINTENANCE

Every year you are in the van, pick a month for cleaning. Spring is a great time for this, when your body naturally wants to begin anew. Take everything out of your van. Everything. And lay it out. Take stock of things that need repair. Do those jobs you've been holding off on now that there isn't anything in the way. And then be strict about letting go of what hasn't been used. You will slowly accumulate things on the road. A T-shirt here, a new mug there, and while those things are wonderful reminders of your travels, we only need so many T-shirts, and in reality, one mug per person. Souvenirs get put in storage to be pulled out when life becomes a little more stationary.

WANTS VS. NEEDS

This concept seems to be a lifelong battle and is only amplified when you have a quarter of the space of a studio apartment. When each item you have is taking up precious space in your already-small living area, it has to have a purpose. Sometimes that purpose is to

---

PROTIP

When we first moved into the van, we didn't have organizational systems in place. This quickly turned into a need. We needed a place to put our dirty shoes when we were done with a hike and our dirty laundry when we had worn the shirt six times in a row. Mostly, we realized we had a lot of gross, smelly things and no place to put them. Don't forget a laundry bag!

CHARLIE

CHARLIE IS THE BASS PLAYER FOR RAPID-GRASS, a high-energy bluegrass band from Colorado. He travels in his van with his bass and enjoys the wilderness in between performances.

VEHICLE
2004 Chevy Express AWD, high top—needed a bass to fit in the vehicle.

CONNECT
@charlesparkermertens

TIME ON THE ROAD
Full-time, 6 months; part-time, 10 years

WORDS OF WISDOM
Since I am an upright-bass player, playing many festivals and concerts around the country and the world, I needed my van to fit the bass. I also wanted all the other van amenities like a tankless shower, electrical system, fridge, sink, and plenty of storage for adventure gear. I had a hell of a time coming up with a design to cram all this stuff together under the bed but am so pleased with the results. It's a micro-apartment on wheels!

I had to give up on the idea of having an enclosed bathroom in order to fit the bass. This can be difficult at times but we don't really have a choice! I plan to add a roof cargo box and possibly a box on a swing-out hitch to be able to fit *more stuff* and bikes.

PROTIP

My tiny van is crammed full of crafts. I sew, mend, macrame, crochet, draw a bit. I'm always making things. This time in my life is for making little things. Less is more, but you've got my blessing to bring all the art supplies. **—KATYA**

SCOTT WOERNER

SCOTT HAD BEEN NOMADIC most of his life and the idea of long stretches of solitude had been a big part of that life. Because of that, he was sure he'd be able to handle the lonely times and lack of fixed roots.

VEHICLE
Ford E350—it was converted into a commercial wheelchair transport van that I modified to load the motorcycle.

CONNECT
@suspicious_white_van

TIME ON THE ROAD
Full-time, 3½ years

CONVERSION
The reason for doing my own build was so I could travel with a motorcycle in the van and still be able to sleep and cook without having to unload it. My whole build revolved around that one requirement. I gave up having a fixed bed for a hammock system. This allows me a lot more flexibility with the moto and has also given me flexibility when looking for level spots to camp.

bring you joy. But often it's more practical. Be kind to yourself and your choices. That's why we have a nonelectric espresso machine and a guitar taking up valuable space. When times are down and the rain is pouring, it's nice to have a hot espresso and a few acoustic tunes for relaxation.

There may be things so important to you, you base your entire van build around them. While our build is based around maximizing storage to travel for our job, there are many others out there who built around different wants and needs.

TRAVEL + THRIVE

chapter 6 LIVE, WORK, STAY CONNECTED

INCOME OPTIONS

TO ENJOY YOUR NEW LIFE OF LONG-TERM TRAVEL (or weekend or seasonal travel), you'll need to have financial resources to support yourself. Even if you plan to outfit a vehicle that you already own, you'll have to purchase materials and spend time building it out. You might still have a vehicle payment. This won't magically disappear once you start living in your vehicle. You'll need money for food, gas, auto insurance, repairs, and general life (I'm looking at you, national park collectible pins). If this feels overwhelming, it's because it is. Flip back to chapter 2 and take a look at our sample budgets to quell the hyperventilating. There are quite a few ways to make ends meet while you're exploring.

OPTION 1: SAVINGS

Save everything you can and travel for as long as you can until that money runs out. This allows for true daily freedom, untethered to Wi-Fi or work hours. We've met plenty of nomads who just planned to adventure until the funds ran out. This option could mean years of saving before moving into your van, depending on how long you want to travel. Cutting spending can be as drastic as selling your house and moving into a smaller apartment, or as relaxed as skipping a meal out each week. Use the budget planner in chapter 2 to get an estimate on what your monthly expenses will be. Give yourself incentives to put more money away with benchmarks and test trips.

Estimated monthly expenses x how many months you want to travel = savings goal

PROTIP

We planned to save enough money to allow us a year on the road without having to work. This plan meant we had to give up any nonessentials (meals out, shopping, etc.) while we were building out the van. We also downsized from renting a house to renting a tiny studio apartment. We did everything we could to save money. We think this really helped with our transition into van life. We learned to live without surplus things and to value experiences over stuff. —NATALIE & ABIGAIL

OPTION 2: FULL-TIME, PART-TIME, CONTRACT WORK

Before moving into a van, we took the savings approach. We saved as much money as we could by selling things we wouldn't need once we lived nomadically (including a car we weren't going to use once we had the van) and renting out our room.

We have been focused in the contract world since moving into a van. We were lucky enough that our first contract required us to travel extensively around the country, so we had a boost into van life. Since then, we've squeezed our way into the freelance writing and photography space—which has sustained us on the road.

There are so many websites that focus on remote work, and many focus on remote work in the outdoor space including:

- Adventure Job Board, adventurejobboard.com
- Flex Jobs, flexjobs.com
- Back Door Jobs, backdoorjobs.com
- SkipTheDrive, skipthedrive.com
- Upwork, upwork.com

More traditional job-search sites, like Indeed and ZipRecruiter, also have "remote" search options.

OPTION 3: TAKE YOUR JOB ON THE ROAD

If you plan to work from the road but don't know where to start, begin with your current job. Is there any way you can do your job from the road? Don't be afraid to pitch your boss the idea of letting you go remote. They may be open to the idea so they don't have to spend time replacing you. We know plenty of modern nomads who have transitioned their work from an office job to a van job.

OPTION 4: RUN (OR START) YOUR OWN BUSINESS FROM THE ROAD

Many full-time van lifers don't only live out of their van, they create out of their van. Some nomads we've met on the road moved into a van to save on overhead costs while they grew their own company. Others profit off of the van life experience, creating YouTube content or selling van-conversion schematics and diagrams. We've also seen nomads who create physical objects—jewelry, art, or clothing, and sell those on e-commerce sites. Starting your own business and running it from the road can be extremely difficult, but also just as rewarding. As your own boss, you can have an income and also decide how your day is set up.

OPTION 5: SEASONAL WORK

Some nomads bounce around from seasonal job to seasonal job. Think ski bums, trail crew, rafting guides, backcountry guides, and park employees. Many of these people live out of their rig and move to another job when the seasons change. It's a great way to blend passions with work habits, while still making enough money to get to the next trailhead.

DEREK REDD

DEREK RUNS GILIGEAR, a sustainable startup centered around eco-conscious, recycled, and long-lasting gear for adventurers. He manages the business from his van.

VEHICLE + WHY
2018 Mercedes-Benz Sprinter—it was the only gray one on the lot. All the white ones lined up had plumber vibes.

CONNECT
@giligear

TIME ON THE ROAD
Full-time, 2 years

WORKING ON THE ROAD
I moved into the van so I could comfortably and efficiently work while traveling and still have enough inventory to run an eco-friendly online business. One of the hardest parts of running my business from the van is work productivity in beautiful places with no Wi-Fi. It's also hard parting ways with new and old friends, and not having my industrial sewing machine with me in the van for creating prototypes.

CASSIE & SCOTT

CASSIE KNEW MOVING INTO A VAN for six months would be an experience they would remember forever. She knew that there would be challenging moments along with beautiful experiences. She was also sure that Scott, her partner, would do most of the driving, and that she would do her best at being the copilot . . . as in trying not to fall asleep fifteen minutes into the journey.

VEHICLE + WHY
2005 Chevy Astro—named Buster. We chose the Astro because of its all-wheel-drive capability, gave it a lift, put on bigger all-terrain tires, and updated several suspension and steering components.

CONNECT
@head.to.tales

TIME ON THE ROAD
Full-time, 6 months

THE PLAN
When we decided to venture out on this six-month van trip, we knew that we wanted to complete some sort of workaway or volunteer program. With those three programs having set dates, the rest of our time we decided to just explore and see what we could see throughout the Northwest and western Canada.

SCOTT HARDESTY & CASSIE WILSON]

THE EXECUTION
Working on the horse ranch in Idaho was eye opening. Our daily activities ranged from feeding the horses to moving pipe to maintaining their lawn and garden. We were two out of six total workaway "helpers" that were staying with this family—a detail that was not communicated to us prior to arrival. We left after two weeks with more understanding about horse breeding and how tough it is (three foals ended up dying in our time there) and about raising cattle and the realities of being a rancher. We went into the ranch in Canada with similar expectations. Upon arrival we were blown away by the differences and welcome we received. This was what we were looking for: animals that were treated with love and respect, a garden overflowing with produce, fresh eggs every morning, fun times riding horses, and friendships of a lifetime.

WORDS OF WISDOM
For anyone looking to do a workaway or other similar program, our biggest advice would be to have plenty of communication prior to your arrival. Ask questions and be specific: Where will you be sleeping? What daily tasks/chores will be expected of you? How many people are living at the residence currently? Will we be expected to work over the weekend? We also relied *heavily* on others' reviews of their experiences on the ranches. Read through these carefully and even consider reaching out to previous workers to chat about their experiences as well.

We spent three summers traveling around the country and setting up a booth at various outdoor and music festivals. We got to know the festival community pretty well. Many of our festival friends were nomadic as well, traveling with the circuit and setting up each weekend. Often, outdoor companies run festival circuits, so this could be an excellent way to continue traveling, though you lose the freedom of choosing where you're going next (this can sometimes be a blessing in disguise).

OPTION 6: FARM STAYS, WWOOFING, WORKAMPING

Farm stays, or finding a WWOOF (World Wide Opportunity on an Organic Farm), is a great way to experience the culture of an area, help a farm that needs extra hands, secure a place to stay, have regular showers, and live on a budget. Most farm stays and WWOOFs trade room and board (a place to sleep and food) for an agreed amount of work a week. We've met van lifers that jump from stay to stay, and those that find a farm and stay for months.

Workamping is the portmanteau of, you guessed it, work and camping. These jobs often come in the form of RV park services and campground hosting. You can make money in these jobs, in addition to having a place to sleep every night. There are a few websites that help connect workampers with places that need assistance—they are a simple internet search away.

OPTION 7: CITY-SPECIFIC WORK AND STAYING IN ONE PLACE WHILE WORKING TEMPORARILY

This is where Craigslist really shines. Craigslist is still a reliable place to find location-specific work, and there is plenty of it. Check out the destination's local Craigslist job board and go from there. It is also possible to find location-specific freelance gigs. This is a great way to get to know a city and give direction to your travels, but not ideal if you need a steady income. City-specific work is unreliable, and stealth camping in cities is difficult long-term.

WORKING FROM YOUR VAN

Most remote jobs require a reliable internet connection. With an unlimited data plan, a smartphone hot spot is the easiest way to work online from your rig. You won't always have enough signal to stream Netflix, but it's usually sufficient for most daily work tasks. A

PROTIP

Working remotely from your computer sounds nice, but if you hit the road you also want to maximize your time in the great outdoors. Try to find a remote job with flexible hours as well—we know, tall order!

cell phone repeater is a wise investment if you need reliable Wi-Fi when off the grid and out of cell service. Once plugged in, this device can boost cell reception for any phone and any carrier. A cell phone repeater doesn't work too far from any cell towers, though, so don't expect a miracle connection in the middle of absolute nowhere.

Strategize and do as much work offline as possible, then upload everything once you reach a reliable connection. Search reviews of cafes in advance to see if a specific coffee

PROTIP

It comes in handy to carry a ten-foot extension cord. Outlet too far from your outside table? You've already got a solution, even if it is a little embarrassing.

THE FOXES

BRANDON AND GABI FOX RUN A PHOTOGRAPHY BUSINESS from their vehicle and visit some of the most beautiful spots in the United States to capture engagements and weddings.

shop or diner will make a suitable workspace. If you show up and it's crowded, buy a coffee and ask for the Wi-Fi password. Assuming you parked as close as possible, you can now go to work from the comfort of your van.

PROTIP

If you plan to work remotely for a company, ask your employer if they will be willing to cover your cell phone bill. If you are a freelancer, you may be able to use your bill as a tax write-off.

VEHICLE + WHY
1972 Airstream—we did a full gut renovation on it to turn it into our dream home on wheels.

CONNECT
@thefoxesphotography/@thefoxstream/@justgoclimb

TIME ON THE ROAD
Full-time, 4 years; now part-time

MAKING THE LEAP
Our reason to hit the road was to pursue a lifestyle of climbing. We left our jobs in Boston to spend a year on the road traveling around the United States and Canada, chasing the good temperatures to climb at world-class destinations.

Then, as will happen, we got hooked on the nomadic lifestyle and decided to keep going! Over the next few years, we kept traveling and figuring out how to make this lifestyle sustainable, eventually starting our photography business, the Foxes Photography.

We remember a specific make-or-break moment when we decided to post up in Washington and really try to make a go at wedding photography out there. If we weren't successful, we were going to move back to Boston and end our life on the road. That really forced us to give it our all and ultimately helped us achieve our goals.

PROTIP

We used cell signals from three different providers. Our primary plan was an unlimited Verizon plan that went to a hot spot. The backup for that was an AT&T unlimited plan also on a hot spot. Then both of our phones were on Google Fi and could get service from either T-Mobile or Sprint. We also used a cellular booster that put an antenna on the roof of the RV that we could use to boost the signal when we were far away from towers. **—NIK & ALLISON WHITE**

chapter 7 NOURISHMENT AND COFFEE

JUST BECAUSE YOU'RE ON THE MOVE doesn't mean you have to settle for truck-stop hot dogs and greasy fast food. With cabinet space at a premium, nomads tend to carry just the kitchen essentials. Start with the staples you use every day. Take a look at chapter 14 for a full checklist.

COOKING OPTIONS

One of our often-asked questions is "What do you eat?" This usually falls just after "Where do you shower?" but before "Where do you sleep?" It's a vital piece to research, plan, and learn as you go.

When we first moved into a van, it took us a while to adjust to cooking in such a small space with limited appliances and utensils. For the first few months, we saved every grocery receipt, figuring out what food went bad, what we ran out of too quickly, how much products cost at different stores, and our favorite meals. What you can cook depends on the cooking setup you've chosen in your rig. There are some who choose to eat only raw and unprocessed food, foregoing a fridge or cooler altogether. We've seen regular coolers, fancy coolers, electric coolers, van fridges, all the way through to industrial sinks and ovens. There are pros and cons to every setup.

FOOD STORAGE

There are many options for food storage in your van, ranging from forgoing any food that requires cold temperatures to installing a full-sized fridge in an RV.

JOHNNY & ELLA

ELLA'S INTEREST IN VAN LIFE BEGAN after hearing about it from a friend who did "car life" in the 1990s. She felt excitement at the thought getting out of the small bubble of New Hampshire that she grew up in. It was a cute, safe bubble, but her soul wanted something different.

Johnny wanted a change from the day-to-day monotony of the past ten years. His then-girlfriend, now wife, Ella, said she wanted to live in a van with or without him. So he said, "If I get to be with you, then yes!"

VEHICLE + WHY
2007 Ford E150 Handicap-Accessible High Top—it was within our budget, reliable, and easy to fix. Ella could stand inside and it had a stealthy exterior.

CONNECT
@expandingexplorers

TIME ON THE ROAD
Full-time, 1 year; part-time, 2 years

COOKING ON THE ROAD
We have been eating vegan in the van for over two years. It started with inspiration from other vegans on YouTube and eating a rainbow of vegetables for health. It also seemed practical to avoid pathogens when we don't have running water in our rig.

A crucial factor in our van build was maximizing our joy of cooking. Multistep meals feel exciting and fulfilling despite the small space. If we aren't outdoors adventuring, then we can be found whipping up plant-based deliciousness in our tiny kitchen. Sure, everything takes a bit longer—but it's worth it to us!

ONLY STORING DRY FOOD

This is possible for short trips or with an aggressive change to your eating style. Most van lifers have some sort of cooling option in their vehicle, but it is possible to live off nuts, dry goods, and packaged food. It just may not be very nutritious or tasty.

STANDARD OR ROTO-MOLDED COOLER

Coolers are a great option for shorter trips. Roto-molded coolers have higher ice-retention times and therefore stay colder for longer. Here are some pros and cons to using a cooler for food storage:

- Requires no energy
- Easily movable around the vehicle
- Ice can melt and ruin food in the water
- Can't store food for more than a few days
- Gambling with food safety when storing meat

12-VOLT FRIDGE

There are a ton of 12v fridge options ranging from five hundred to thousands of dollars.

- Two options: chest-style refrigerators and upright front-loading
- Holds enough food for at least ten days away from a grocery store
- Low power draw
- Expensive
- More moving parts, more possibility to break

PROTIP

Shy away from any 120-volt dorm-style fridge. They aren't energy efficient enough for true off-grid living and they're not made to withstand lots of vibrations like they'll experience while you're driving.

SAMPLE VAN MEALS

What you can make in a house with two burners, you can make in a van. It all depends on how much preparation and cleanup you want to do. Below we will outline options ranging from some of our fanciest meals (most ingredients, most time) to some of our quickest, easiest favorites (fastest, least ingredients), including vegetarian, gluten-free, and dairy-free options.

HAMBURGERS + VEGGIES

Servings: 2
Prep time: 10 min.
Cook time: 15 min.

Ingredients

- **PREMADE HAMBURGER PATTIES:** We usually get two at a time to reduce the amount of raw meat in our fridge at any time. Most grocery stores will make patties for you at their meat counter, or you can grab two premade patties. The goal is to easily transfer them straight to the cast iron without having to form the patties and touch raw meat in the back/side/front country. These can be substituted with veggies burgers.
- **BUNS:** Gluten-free options are available at most grocery stores. If not, we grab a few pieces of gluten-free bread or use large pieces of lettuce.
- **CONDIMENTS:** Ketchup, mustard, aioli. We usually already have these things in our fridge.

- **PICKLES:** Always.
- **SIDE VEGGIE:** Brussels sprouts, broccoli, carrots, sweet potato fries, or grab whatever needs to get eaten before it goes bad
- **CHEESE:** Anything from American Cheese slices to gourmet gouda.
- **FAT OF CHOICE:** Butter, coconut oil, ghee, olive oil, sesame oil, etc.

Cooking Instructions

1. Rinse and cut the veggies. Cook those in your first pan over medium heat with your fat of choice, salt, and pepper. Timing will depend on the vegetable. Start with 5 minutes, and taste-test as you go until you get to your desired consistency.
2. Throw two burgers on your second pan/cast iron with a fat of your choice.
3. Burgers will need to be flipped after 6 to 7 minutes on low heat. Don't touch them until then—letting them sear will keep in the flavor.
4. Flip, cook the other side (5 to 6 minutes), and also throw the buns on for a little toasting. It might be the magic of the cast iron, but usually everything is ready around the same time.
5. Build your burger, and enjoy it.

CHICKEN QUESADILLAS

Servings: 2
Prep time: 10 min.
Cook time: 15 min.

Ingredients

- ½ jar salsa: Make another round later with the other half.
- ½ can refried beans: Or any beans.
- Shredded or ground chicken: Three-quarter pounds for a meal for two. If you're going vegetarian, substitute avocado or a hearty veggie.
- Tortillas: Or chips if you just want to dip.
- Hot sauce
- Cheese: If you're a dairy fan.
- Fat of choice: Butter, coconut oil, ghee, olive oil, sesame oil, etc.
- Veggies: Anything that might go bad soon. Peppers, onion, etc.

Cooking Instructions

1. Combine refried beans and salsa in cast iron with a generous amount of the fat of your choice. Some will say adding acid to your cast iron isn't best "cast iron practice," but if you continue to use it and season it, it's going to be just fine.
2. Brown chicken in other cast iron.
3. Add chicken to refried beans–salsa mix. Add in extra veggies if you have them.
4. Crisp tortillas on newly empty cast iron.
5. Add cheese to crisp tortillas and melt.
6. Build your quesadillas, and enjoy.

BREAKFAST SCRAMBLE

Servings: 2
Prep time: 5 min.
Cook time: 15 min.

Ingredients

- Eggs
- Sausage (precooked): Optional, or find vegetarian sausage.
- Fat of choice: Butter, coconut oil, ghee, olive oil, sesame oil, etc.
- Veggies: Anything that might go bad soon. Peppers, onion, etc.
- Salsa: Optional.
- Leftovers

Cooking Instructions

1. Put fat of choice and veggies (always salt and pepper) in cast iron first, let them cook.
2. Add eggs on top and scramble in pan.
3. Pile eggs on top of bread or tortilla from the night before.
4. Enjoy.

CONNIE

EVER SINCE SHE WENT ON HER FIRST OUT-DOOR CLIMBING TRIP, she started dreaming about climbing full-time. Just as she was ready to shelve that dream for good in lieu of a great job and supportive community, her partner convinced her to hit the road.

VEHICLE + WHY
Red 2003 Freightliner Sprinter—we inherited it from my partner's parents. It's in dire need of a paint job.

CONNECT
@conniesaurus.rex

TIME ON THE ROAD
Full-time, 1 year

COOKING ON THE ROAD
Necessity is the mother of invention! My partner and I both have a sweet tooth, so I started experimenting right away with making treats with our camp stove. I started a blog with tips for how to bake on a stove-top. Here is one of my

CONNIE SHANG

favorites: brown butter chocolate-chip skillet cookie. This is a camping classic to master by heart. When you're mixing ingredients by hand, you have to melt the butter, so you might as well brown it for that extra caramelized, nutty goodness.

BROWN BUTTER CHOCOLATE CHIP SKILLET COOKIE

Servings: 8
Prep time: 10 min.
Cook time: 12 min.

Ingredients

- 6 tablespoons butter
- 1 scant cup white sugar
- 1 large egg
- 1 teaspoon vanilla extract
- 1 cup all-purpose flour, spooned and leveled
- ½ teaspoon baking soda
- ½ teaspoon flaky sea salt
- ½ cup chocolate chips

Cooking Instructions

1. Melt butter in a heavy-bottomed nonstick 10-inch skillet on medium-low heat. To brown the butter, scrape the bottom frequently with a rubber spatula, about 5 minutes. Butter will start to foam. When the butter starts to turn golden brown and smell nutty, remove from heat and set aside.

2. While butter is browning, beat sugar, egg, and vanilla extract in a large mixing bowl until smooth. Stir in flour, baking soda, salt, and brown butter and mix until it forms a dough.

3. Spread dough evenly across the skillet. Sprinkle chocolate chips over the cookie dough.

4. Cover tightly with a preheated heavy lid and cook on low heat for 12 minutes or until it smells fragrant. If the cookie isn't done, turn off the heat and let the cookie continue to cook in the residual heat, but do not let it overcook. Slice and serve hot, or dig in with a fork.

Tips

- If you overcook the butter, there will be lots of brown specks from the caramelized milk solids. This isn't bad, except that your cookies will have brown specks in them.
- Instead of mixing chocolate chips into the dough, I find that sprinkling them over the top prevents them from sinking to the bottom.
- This one will take some experimenting and luck to get the timing just right, but it's totally worth it.

MORNING COFFEE

There are many ways to make a steaming (or iced) cup of delicious coffee in a van. Preference for how it's brewed is as eclectic as the ways you can make it. Start experimenting!

FRENCH PRESS

The French press method is both simple and easy, however, convenience comes with a price. Since you need coarse ground coffee, your final product won't be quite as complex as some other brewing methods.

PROS

- Straightforward brewing process
- Brews the most coffee (depending on the size of your French press)
- Durable. We use a stainless-steel French press that has taken a beating and still functions.

CONS

- Requires some cleanup. The grounds clump to the bottom of the press and they can be challenging to get out.
- Takes up space. A French press takes up the most space compared to the other brewing options listed here.

AEROPRESS

Much like an espresso machine, the AeroPress uses pressure to force water through coffee grounds. As a result, the AeroPress makes a really strong cup of coffee. It's not quite espresso, but this brewing method does have a bold flavor. The AeroPress requires a finely ground coffee.

PROS

- The AeroPress is small and doesn't take up as much space as a French press.
- AeroPress makes a strong cup of coffee.
- It's fast and easy. With this method, there isn't any waiting or timing needed.

CONS

- It's plastic. If pouring hot water into plastic makes you uncomfortable, this may not be for you.
- It requires special filters.
- It only makes one cup of coffee at a time.

POUR-OVER

Pour-over coffee can have a huge range in complexity and taste. It's an easy method that, with a little know-how, can produce a phenomenal cup of coffee. If you are making a pour-over, grind your coffee to medium-fine.

PROS

- Simplicity. You only need one item to make it and you brew it directly into your mug.
- Easy cleanup.
- Best taste. If done right, pour-over coffee will be rich, smooth, and complex.

CONS

- Getting the perfect brew requires time and timing. You must pour the water over the coffee in intervals.
- Pouring the hot water can be complicated. It's easier with a gooseneck kettle.
- If not done correctly, the coffee can be weak.

CLEANUP

Cleaning up a van-cooked meal can be a dirty topic, but with practice, you'll learn to cut down on your mess. Keep both a trash and a recycling option in your vehicle. Use as few dishes as possible as you cook, and clean your space as you go.

Always try to Leave No Trace. LNT is the practice of leaving a space better than you found it and having a low impact on the natural areas around you. Throwing out food scraps or leaving trash in an area is extremely harmful to the surrounding ecosystem. Protect the wildlife and yourself by keeping everything contained in your van. You can often get rid of trash at gas stations, camping areas (with permission), and national parks. National parks are also great places to offload recyclables.

chapter 8 VAN LIFE BASICS

IT TAKES TIME TO FIND YOUR RHYTHM ON THE ROAD. Start smart by learning some basic strategies and skills.

We often joke that our life is half adventure and half logistics. Planning is one of the biggest time vacuums. Where do we go next? Where will we sleep? How much water until we run dry? Where is the nearest grocery store? Do you think that couple with the nicer van will let us use their shower?

PROTIP

Decision fatigue is real. When faced with too many decisions, the brain will shut down and stop weighing pros and cons. Sometimes decision fatigue causes you to refuse to make a choice at all. Avoid decision fatigue by starting with an overall plan you can follow loosely. You can also eliminate decisions from other parts of your life in order to have more focus—plan out your meals in advance, simplify your wardrobe, or decide to stay in one place for an extended time.

BOONDOCKING 101:
HOW TO FIND A FREE CAMPSITE

You'd think finding a great free campsite is just an internet search and a bumpy dirt road away, but it's never that simple. Boondocking, also known as dispersed camping, free camping, or dry camping, is the art of finding a quiet place on public lands to park your rig and camp under the stars for free. Your neighbors are critters (that sometimes make their way into your van—hello raccoon friend who decided our van pantry was a far better food source than the forest floor; to be fair, it was) and your backyard view is calming. Where you'll be traveling, geographically speaking, will play a huge part in how difficult it is to find free camping. If you're on the East Coast, it's a lot more challenging to find free spots than on the western side of the country where public land is plentiful and expansive. There are different ways to approach finding a spot, and through experience and research, you'll figure out the best approach for you.

JUST A NIGHT

When long-distance traveling, standards for single-night stopovers lower. These times are when it might be best to find a Walmart parking lot (check ahead of time that they allow overnight camping, as some have banned it) or a quick pull-off on a secondary road.

Paying for a campground, though they can be crowded and sometimes noisy, is also a good option for a quick night stopover. Campground expenses can add up, so avoid them for extended camping trips.

BASECAMP

A basecamp for extended stays warrants higher standards. Look for semi-accessible locations that you'll want to return to over and over again after adventuring in the area, and a great view. Who doesn't want to fall asleep and wake up to a stunning view?

Tools to Help Find Basecamp

iOverlander is a smartphone-based app that utilizes user-sourced data to track free campsites. It's geared more toward people in their vehicles and less toward people looking for a nice place to pitch a tent. The app can indicate (depending on the information provided by the user) if dogs are allowed, if there is cell service and on what provider, and if there are any other amenities.

The website freecampsites.net works in a similar fashion. There are plenty of apps that have lists of free campsites—Campendium and FreeRoam are two others. Granted, since they are user-sourced applications, they are not where we stop our searching. There is so much more available camping than what will appear on these platforms. If you decide to find a spot using one of these platforms, remember the user is just pointing you to a single spot. Usually, you'll drive down a road that's full of camping spots before you reach the one marked on the app. Don't be afraid to explore. Just pay attention to the description and whether the user recommends having a high-clearance vehicle or 4x4 to reach the pinned camping spot.

If you want to get a little more adventurous and find your own spot, look no further than one of our country's greatest assets: public land. If you're out on an adventure, more than likely you will find yourself near mountains, beaches, and deserts. Many of our nation's national parks are surrounded by public land that is open for camping. Camping rules vary from region to region so do your research ahead of time. BLM (Bureau of Land Management)—managed land, for example, allows camping off of most secondary roads (i.e., nonpaved), and you can also legally camp on many forest service roads. You can use

free mapping software from CalTopo to show you where private land ends and public lands begin. The FreeRoam site and app allow you to overlay BLM land, cell service areas, and US Forest Service (USFS) land on the map as you search. You need to be comfortable with reading maps if you go this route, but it can be very beneficial for finding epic campsites.

Avenza Maps is also another popular mapping software. With Avenza Maps you can actually download free BLM and USFS "Motor Vehicle Use Maps" or "MVUMs" that will show you where you are allowed to drive. You can filter your search to areas near you, or look nearby your potential destination. Navigate to the legend and look for an indicator for "Dispersed Camping." This will allow you to find incredible campsites that aren't as popular as the ones listed on other websites and apps.

You need to camp in an area that has been camped in before. You cannot damage natural resources by creating a new campsite. Sometimes, even though a road on a map is marked as "dispersed camping allowed," there might not be any established campsites. In this case, Google Maps can be a powerful tool. If you find a road you'd like to camp on but don't want to risk driving down a rutted-out dirt road for thirty minutes only to get skunked,

look at the road up close using the satellite view on Google Maps. One limitation is that you won't be able to see camping spots if the road has heavy tree cover. You also won't be able to assess the condition of the road.

It's also possible to sleep at trailheads that aren't marked with "No overnight parking" signs. There is sometimes access to a pit toilet, and it's a great way to get an early jump on the next day's adventure. Usually, if you can backpack from the trailhead, it's perfectly legal to sleep at that trailhead overnight.

PROTIP

Don't be afraid to stop in the local ranger station and ask for dispersed-camping recommendations. The rangers are always friendly and happy to point you to a great legal place to set up basecamp.

URBAN CAMPING

Finding a quick place to sleep in town can be a bit more challenging. In some cities you can still legally sleep in a vehicle. However, many large cities have banned it so take a look at each city's individual laws. This doesn't apply when sleeping on private property.

Rest stops are a great place to sleep. They usually have an eight-hour limit to prevent people from overstaying their welcome, but they have access to 24-hour bathrooms.

Big-name retailers like Walmart and Safeway often lend their parking lots to weary travelers. Stop in and chat with a manager before assuming they do—not all locations allow overnight parking and you might be awakened by an angry security guard, police officer, or tow truck driver. Like retailers, some truck stops have overnight parking as well. It's best to be clean, quiet, and courteous to minimize the risk of being asked to move.

GETTING DOWN TO BUSINESS: WHERE TO GO #2

Let's talk about bathroom logistics. It's not quite as complicated as people make it out to be.

When you actually pay attention to them, bathrooms are everywhere: gas stations, grocery stores, campgrounds, trailheads, hotel lobbies, etc. Without a toilet in your vehicle,

you can work bathroom breaks into travel time and camp in areas where there are pit toilets in the vicinity. Carry a shovel in case nature calls and there are no other options around. If your solution is to bury your number two, make sure you follow the LNT basics.

- Bury your waste at least six inches deep.
- Don't do your business within three hundred feet of a water source.
- Always pack out your toilet paper, even if it says it's compostable.

There is a case to be made for installing a toilet in your rig. This will likely be determined by your lifestyle, where you will be traveling, and your comfort level using public bathrooms.

KEEP IT CLEAN

It is possible to build a shower into your vehicle. Whether you want to or not is entirely up to your wants, needs, and budget. There are plenty of ways to wash without a fully functioning shower if you are willing to get creative and potentially step outside of your comfort zone.

When we first began our nomadic lifestyle, we fit the classic dirtbag model. We'd shower a couple of times a week at best. We'd take dips in every lake and stream we could find. This will work for a lot of people, but what we found is that when we went to bed dirty, our sheets would hold all of that dust and dirt that was falling off of us while we slept. Everyone is different in this regard, but for long-term travel, we found that we needed a way to bathe at least semi-regularly to maintain the enjoyment level that we had come to expect from our travels. If you've decided not to install a permanent shower in your vehicle, below are some creative ways to keep clean when living an otherwise dirty lifestyle.

TRUCK STOPS

We modern nomads can learn a lot from the great American wayfarers: long-haul truckers. Truckers often live in their cabs for weeks on end. Truck stops can be an oasis. Hot showers, complete with towels, soap, and a blow-dryer, are at most of the big-name truck stops, though they can be a little pricey. Cut down on costs by joining a loyalty program if one is available. Expect to pay between $10 and $20 for a hot shower at a truck stop, but you'll also get a clean place to wash off that may even feel luxurious.

Campground

Yes, if you pay to camp in a developed campground, there is a chance that the campground will have showers (sometimes hot). If you are feeling dirty and you find yourself near a developed campground, feel free to ask the campground host if they would be willing to sell you a shower. Sometimes the showers are coin-operated and the host will just point you in the right direction. Other times they might ask for a $5 per-person fee for a hot shower. The types of showers, and how desirable they are, will vary wildly from campground to campground. We've found showers in immaculate, clean, private buildings where we've almost felt at home. On the flip side, we've showered in moldy spider-infested showers that almost had us running out of there screaming. Almost.

POOLS, AQUATIC CENTERS, AND COMMUNITY RECREATION CENTERS

Nothing beats a shower and some hot-tub time after a long day of backcountry skiing in the winter. Yes, we said hot tub. You don't have to be a member of most rec centers to use the facilities—the price will depend on the location. Some places will let you shower (and give you a clean towel) for $5, and others will let you use the entire facility for the same price. Even small towns tend to have rec centers that are open to the public, and you'll leave feeling like you just had a day at the spa . . . a van life spa!

GYMS

A popular option for modern nomads is to buy a gym membership from a facility with multiple locations. Many of these gyms are open twenty-four hours a day and have excellent showers. As a bonus, you can keep up with your workout routine. Memberships can be very cheap, as little as $20 per person per month.

LAUNDRY DAY

Many apartment owners face the same issue when it comes to laundry: no room for a washer and dryer. Laundromats often have Wi-Fi, and some even have showers. Take laundry time as a chance to get both your clothes and hopefully yourself clean, and then catch up on a bit of work.

There's also always the "handwash and hang dry" option. Or a combination of the two—wash everything at a Laundromat, then take the wet clothes to the campsite and hang them up. We have gotten into trouble with this a few times, with clothes flying everywhere or caterpillars descending from the trees directly onto our drying clothes.

MAIL CALL

If you give up your permanent address, you're going to run into a few hiccups. Forgoing a permanent residence will affect many things, including your taxes, vehicle insurance, health insurance, where you can receive mail, and voting. Our advice is to ask friends or family members to use their address as your main mailing and living address. You can also set up a forwarding address to a different legal permanent residence in a more "nomadic friendly" state. This is called establishing a new domicile. There are three states that are pretty friendly for this, having low taxes, ease of getting necessary documents, and great mail forwarding companies. Start your research with South Dakota, Texas, and Florida, then go from there.

There are several alternatives to having your friends or family forward your mail while you're traveling. The US Postal Service (USPS) will accept packages and letters and hold them for free if they are delivered via general delivery. Address the package like so:

Name
General Delivery
City, State Zip (of the USPS office)

The post office will hold the package (for thirty days) until you arrive with a valid form of identification. If you will be around a certain US post office for a while, you can set up a PO box at that location. This can be done online. There is also the option to set up boxes at FedEx or UPS.

It's possible to receive mail on the road in other ways that require a little more foresight and planning. Often, campgrounds will accept packages for you, although check ahead of time to make sure they don't charge a fee. Sometimes, if we know we are staying at an Airbnb, we will chat with the owner and have a package delivered to that address.

TOPPING OFF THE WATER TANK

The logistics of getting water will depend on what type of holding tanks you use in your vehicle. Portable tanks work well because they are easier to fill up and don't require a hose from a water source to the van. There are also some pretty cool custom water tanks out there that can be placed permanently around the wheel well of your rig to conserve space. The only downside here is that you'll need a hose to fill it up.

Much like finding a campsite, you can use the iOverlander app to access user-sourced data to help find free water sources. That is a good place to start, but oftentimes the water sources listed on the app aren't all that convenient. Don't wait until you are completely out of water to re-up. Anytime there is access to free water sources, fill up the holding tanks (and solar shower if you have it). You can find free water in many state and national parks. More often than not, you don't even have to pay the entry fee to access free water. Usually, the water spigot is near the visitor center. You can find free water at some truck stops and gas stations as well. Some states like California even require gas stations to offer free air and drinking water to the public. When you're filling your gas tank, take a look near the air compressor—that's usually where you'll find a free water hookup.

In a pinch, don't be afraid to ask a gear shop or coffee shop if they have a hose or sink where you could top off your water.

PROTIP

A Water Bandit connects to an unthreaded or stripped faucet of any size on one side and has a standard hose connection on the other. Carry one along with a short section of hose to access hard-to-reach water sources or connect without standard threading. If all else fails and you can't find free water, most grocery stores have water refill stations inside for a few cents a gallon. Don't be afraid to walk your water tanks in and fill up. We've even filled our solar shower up in a grocery store before (and paid on our way out).

If and how you decide to filter water is entirely up to you and your comfort level with drinking potentially contaminated water. If you get your water from reverse osmosis water refill stations in grocery stores, then you won't need to bother with an extra filter. To be safe, we always filter the water before it goes into our tanks. While this can be helpful in keeping your water safe to drink, it can also improve your water's taste. As a last resort, we always have our backcountry supplies with us in the van. That includes both a Sawyer water filter and a Grayl GeoPress. If we're in the middle of an adventure and finding water isn't an option, we can at least filter water for drinking.

chapter 9 STAY SAFE, STAY SANE

IN THIS CHAPTER WE'LL COVER SOME EXTRAS that you might want to carry with you to help if something goes sideways. We'll also cover some ways to keep *yourself* healthy—both mentally and physically. Full-time travel is both rewarding and exhausting. When we have bad days, there's nowhere to hide and no privacy to regroup. Bad days can start with a flat tire, a wrong turn, or a snarky comment that turns into a full-blown fight. We've lived through the ups and downs and we've got some helpful tips to help keep your relationship with your partner, family, van-buddy, and yourself rolling smoothly as you travel across the landscape.

KEEP YOUR VEHICLE SAFE

The only certainty during constant travel is uncertainty. Keeping a few items on hand to help in case you accidentally get your rig stuck in the mud thirty miles from civilization can be the difference between a minor inconvenience and a dangerous situation.

SAFETY GEAR

The more you travel, the more you will have the opportunity to work on your problem-solving skills—lucky you! During our first year on the road, it seemed like things went wrong on a daily basis. Looking back, we were clearly unprepared and unequipped to deal with many of the problems we faced. It's best to stay ahead of the game so you can make it to your next destination safely and easily. Some of the items we carry onboard serve dual purposes, like our personal locator beacon (PLB), which is used for backpacking and backcountry travel but would also come in handy should we have an emergency situation outside of cell service. We've never had to use some of the gear and hope to

never use it in the future. But they bring peace of mind and will be helpful should something disastrous happen.

Fire Extinguisher

Carrying a fire extinguisher is a must. They're small, inexpensive, and might save your life. The last thing we want is an accidental fire inside our home, a home that happens to be attached to tanks of gasoline and propane. Fire extinguishers come in different types and are designed to put out different types of fires. They're designated by the letters A, B, C, D, and K. They also make hybrid fire extinguishers like the ABC fire extinguisher. An ABC dry chemical extinguisher is designed to put out fires in the A-class (wood, cloth, rubber, and many plastics), the B-class (flammable liquids, gases, and greases), and C-class (fires involving energized electrical equipment). These are the most common fires you're likely to encounter in a van. They're also good to have on hand if you have a fire at your campsite. Starting a wildfire would be worse than setting your van on fire. Unless you did both.

Small Shovel

Speaking of fire, having a shovel onboard can really come in handy. They're inexpensive and they serve multiple purposes. A small light-duty shovel can be used to cover your hot campfire coals with dirt, dig a toilet with a view, help level your van at night, and dig your tires out if you get stuck in the mud or snow.

Carbon Monoxide and Explosive Gas Detector

If your setup allows for cooking in the van, or if you're using any type of propane or gas, carry a carbon monoxide and explosive gas detector. It will alert you to the presence of harmful gases inside your van. The signs of carbon monoxide poisoning are not always obvious and the cost of the detector is low. Golden rule? If you start hallucinating, get to fresh air, and get a detector—stat.

PROTIP

To avoid the buildup of carbon monoxide when cooking inside, always have fresh air circulating in your vehicle.

Tool Kit

No matter how sturdy you think your vehicle and build-out is, things will break, come loose, and need repairs. Having a basic tool kit (start with a basic kit from a hardware store) will help you out in these situations. Being able to fix things on your own time instead of urgently running into town to buy a specific tool will save you more than a few headaches.

Tow Strap

A tow strap is one of those "just in case" kind of items. We've never actually had to use ours. Make no mistake, we've gotten our van stuck (twice, actually), and both times we did not have a tow strap. Luckily for us, we didn't have to wait too long before a jacked-up rock crawler drove by and offered to pull us out with their tow strap. They love doing that. Now, we carry our own so if we do get stuck, we can at least offer a tow strap if we are fortunate enough to have someone stop to offer help.

Adequate Tires

It doesn't matter what you get as long as it's appropriate for the conditions you plan to drive in. If you will be in the mountains all winter, it might be worth investing in a dedicated set of snow tires. Snow-tire technology has come a long way in recent years and you might be surprised by how effective they can be. Snow tires are made with a softer

rubber compound and shouldn't be driven in warmer weather. Since we didn't have room in our budget for two sets of tires, we went with the best compromise, mountain- and snow-rated all-terrain tires.

Tire Chains and/or Kitty Litter (Winter Only)

If you plan to travel in snowy conditions, particularly in the mountains, consider carrying a set of tire chains or a bag of kitty litter. Both of these items can help when things get slippery. Chains won't do much if you're already stuck, but kitty litter will! It's helped us out of a bad spot more than once. Throw it down under your drive tires to gain traction in a slippery situation.

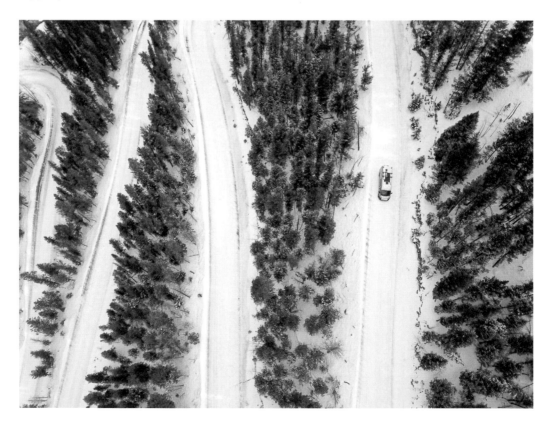

Spare Tire in Good Condition and a Working Jack

Do yourself a favor and inspect your spare regularly to make sure you can use it if you need to. Jacks can be accidentally built into the van so they are inaccessible (also something we've experienced). Make sure both items are in working order before heading off on an adventure.

Air Compressor

If something happens and you get a tire leak in an area that isn't conducive for changing a tire, like a rocky forest-service road, you can use a small air compressor to top off your tire until you make it to a better location. You can also use a compressor to "air down" and reinflate your tires if you will be driving on sand.

Jumper Cables

Breaking down is never fun, but it's better when you have the tools available to help get yourself back on the grid. If your battery dies, it will be much easier to find someone to give you a jump if you have the jumper cables and know how to use them. It's obvious, but it's worth saying that red (on the battery and the jumper cables) is positive and black (or any other color) is negative. Connect the positive cables to the positive terminals and connect the negative cables to the negative terminals.

Roadside Assistance
Being a member of a roadside assistance program like AAA is always a good fallback option. It will save you money if you need a tow.

Second Key/Key Fob
While not mandatory by any means, we *strongly* recommend carrying a second key. If you feel safe doing so, you can buy a magnetic lockbox that can be hidden somewhere under your vehicle. If not, you can lock it inside your vehicle and have someone like AAA pick your lock so you can gain access to your second key. Once upon a time, while on a press trip in upstate South Carolina, one of us, not naming any names (it was Ben), dropped our only electronic key fob into a very deep lake—the fob was gone forever. Having a locksmith get you into your vehicle is one thing, but we had to find a locksmith who could make a laser-cut key and program it to actually work in our van. This proved to be an extremely difficult and expensive operation in such a rural area. It could have been avoided if we had a second key with us.

TRAVELING THROUGH THE SEASONS
If you plan on spending winters in the mountains, or in any other area with cold and snowy weather, be prepared and carry a few extra items to keep you rolling. Winter presents a whole host of additional challenges that you might not immediately consider. For example, finding camping is significantly more difficult. Many forest service roads are closed or impassable due to snow. Winter really isn't the time to go exploring deep in the wilderness unless your rig is adequately equipped. We rely heavily on sleeping at trailheads in the winter. It's much nicer to use a pit toilet than to drop your pants in a snowstorm.

Depending on how cold it gets, your water lines and holding tanks might freeze. There are some options for keeping your system from freezing solid and then exploding. You can purchase 12v heating pads for your tanks and water lines, but anything with a heating element will drain your battery fairly quickly. You'll probably encounter less sunshine in the winter, so if you have solar be mindful of how it is behaving in the colder months.

PROTIP

We disconnect our sink and drain the water lines at night in the cold months when we won't be in the van and running our heater. We've had two separate faucets freeze and explode during a cold snap.

ODDS AND ENDS

These items won't quite save your life—but they might save you a little time and aggravation.

Gear Ties

You may have seen Gear Ties at the hardware store. They're made by Nite Ize and serve as a heavy-duty reusable zip tie. We use them to secure things, hang things, organize cords—the list is endless.

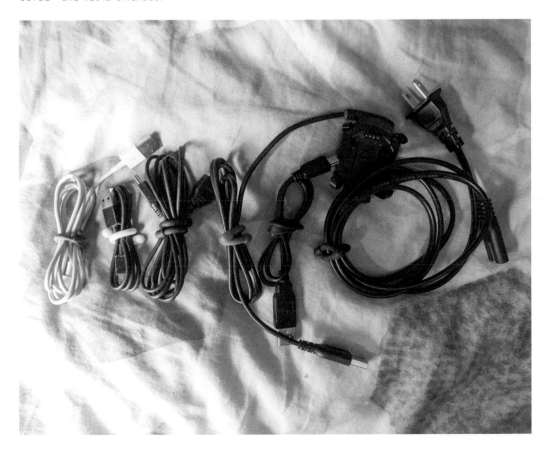

Heavy-Duty Tape/Adhesive

Heavy-duty tape like Gorilla Tape or duct tape and superglue are always great to have on hand for quick fixes around your rig. Teflon tape is also a good idea for any quick plumbing fixes that you might need to make on the go.

Hatchet

A hatchet helps with collecting firewood or splitting small logs. It's also great for looking like you belong in the woods.

A Tarp and Paracord

A few lengths of paracord and a tarp work well for building a makeshift shelter. This is a perfectly acceptable way to create some shade and shield yourself from the sun and rain.

Doormat

A doormat might seem a little ridiculous, but it's a great way to keep dirt out of the van. Any mat will do, but we use an eco-friendly sand-free mat made from recycled material. It allows the dust and sand to fall through rather than collecting all of that debris on top.

Extra Fuses

A little more practical than some of our odds and ends is a box of extra fuses. You can grab them at any auto parts store, and they'll be really great to have if/when you blow a fuse in your rig.

KEEP YOURSELF SAFE

As the second-most important item on Maslow's Hierarchy of Needs, feeling safe in your own home is a top priority. It can be much harder to feel safe when your home has a lot of doors and windows and four wheels. The items listed above are helpful for keeping your van safe, but how do you go about keeping yourself physically safe?

Living in a vehicle, especially solo, can make you feel vulnerable. This is particularly true in larger cities with high crime rates. It's worth noting that our time on the road has somewhat restored our faith in humanity. We have been helped countless times by complete strangers and we are fortunate to have never been harmed or threatened.

FIND CAMP BEFORE DARK

If at all possible, when traveling in a new area, find camp before dark. This is extra important if you think that you'll be traveling off the main road. It allows you to get a lay of the land before the sun goes down.

LOCK UP

Lock your doors and roll your windows up far enough so that someone can't reach through the window and unlock the door.

BE CAREFUL WHEN ANSWERING LATE-NIGHT KNOCKS

Ideally, you should never have a knock in the middle of the night unless you've camped somewhere that's prohibited. If someone knocks on your home in the middle of the night, take a second to try to figure out if it is an actual police officer before opening a door.

PROTIP

I'm no braver than you. I just simply got the dang thing and left in it. Take all the precaution you can, be prepared, but do not overthink it. Just go for it! I have never run into *any* problems because I'm a solo woman. I stay aware of my surroundings and pay attention to everything. But I had to do the same thing before living in a van so nothing really changed. It's no different than being a solo woman going anywhere these days. **—SYDNEY FERBRACHE**

LAURA EDMONDSON

LAURA HAD LIVED THE VAN LIFE ONCE BEFORE, but only temporarily. This time around she was ready to put all of the pieces into place: a job that let her work remotely, the right van for the right price, and a lease about to end.

VEHICLE + WHY
2013 Ford Transit Connect—it is the newest model of this particular body style, it gets great gas mileage for a camper van, and it was less expensive to both buy and build out.

CONNECT
@laura.edmondson

TIME ON THE ROAD
Full-time, 1 year

JANELLE PACIENCIA

WORDS OF WISDOM

1. Keep your exact location to yourself (don't post it on the 'gram) until after you've left, *but* always tell at least one person where you're staying in case of emergencies.

2. Be prepared to sacrifice scenery for security. Just because the view in the morning will be beautiful doesn't mean it's a safe place to park overnight.

3. Always keep your gas tank at least one-quarter full so you can leave and put some distance between yourself and a sketchy situation if necessary.

ON MANAGING CRISES
The hardest part of van life for me is managing all the unexpected things that come up. From my dog getting sick to having to get my transmission replaced on my way home for Christmas, life on the road pulls no punches. The best advice I could've given myself before starting on this journey is to accept that those big things will happen outside of my control and the only thing I can do about them is to keep moving forward.

HOW TO KEEP IT GOING
I work remotely as a digital educator on Instagram, a podcast host, a Diversity and Inclusion consultant, public speaker, and as the Corporate Responsibility Manager for Brown Girls Climb. All of these roles add up and keep my lifestyle tenable while still allowing me the flexibility that I have always wanted.

KATYA

KATYA ENDED A LONG-TERM RELATIONSHIP and wanted to take her time deciding where to land next. She'd followed the tiny house movement for a very long time and her ideas and expectations had evolved. When it came down to it, a van was her only logical choice. It was time for a good old-fashioned American road trip.

VEHICLE + WHY
2012 Ford Transit Connect—it was the biggest, squarest mini–cargo van in my price range. I've envied friends' palatial setups, but boy do I like parking effortlessly and gas lasting forever.

CONNECT
@katyacreepin

TIME ON THE ROAD
Full-time, a year and a half

WORDS OF WISDOM
I keep my head up and am ready for trouble, but trouble seems to know better. There are things I don't do, risks I avoid, but that's the cost of doing business as a woman wherever you are.

As for pros, I guess no one sees me as a threat so doors fall open everywhere. I feel very strongly that traveling alone is the only way to be really open to possibilities and adventure and I wouldn't trade it for company or security—well maybe, but he'd have to be extremely cute and useful.

I often really wish I had a window, but I don't know if I would change it. Stealth has been by far the biggest factor in how safe and comfortable I've felt on the road and a window would cost me that.

Usually, if an officer is going to knock, they will light your van up with the spotlight on their car. This is a good indicator that it's a police officer and not an intruder. Before you open your door, make sure they identify themselves. Look out the window to make sure they're in uniform. If you still feel unsafe, call 911 or the nonemergency response number in the area and inform them of the situation.

ADDITIONAL SECURITY

If you find that you are still not sleeping soundly at night, and you think some extra security would help, there are additional measures you can take. Add deadbolts to your doors, add a metal cage between your cockpit and cargo area, and/or install wireless CCTV cameras on the outside of your van. Most of that is probably overkill unless you plan to be urban camping. Our main alarm system is our dog, Henry.

PERSONAL SAFETY ITEMS

Portable Water Filters
Great to have just in case, and if you head off for a backpacking trip.

Personal Locator Beacon
A PLB is primarily used in the backcountry. It doubles as a GPS messaging device with an SOS feature. If there was a serious emergency out of cell service, it can be used to call for help.

First-Aid Kit
Carry two—a larger one with plenty of supplies for travel, and a smaller backcountry kit.

Headlamp
Headlamps are great for any time you need light but also need your hands. They're perfect for working on things outside the van at night. They're also great for any nighttime outdoor activity like hiking.

Fire Starter/Storm-Proof Matches
In case you need to start a fire in a pinch.

PERSONAL SAFETY GEAR CHECKLIST
- ❍ Portable water filter
- ❍ Personal locator beacon
- ❍ First-aid kit
- ❍ Headlamp
- ❍ Fire starter/storm-proof matches

KEEP YOURSELF SANE

Mental health is a huge component of van life. Sometimes it's the impetus to move into a van in the first place. Once you're in the van, there are often high highs and low lows. It can be lonely and disconnected, even if you happen to be with a partner. Luckily, there are plenty of ways to stay connected, find help, and support those valid feelings. We are neither mental health professionals nor doctors so please consider this advice as simply words to the wise. If you are having serious issues, please seek professional help immediately.

REMOTE THERAPISTS

If funds allow and you're in an area with good service, you can seek therapy via online remote sessions. There are plenty of options an internet search away that are easily accessible and affordable. This can be a great way to stay on top of your mental health while you're on the road.

REMOTE DOCTORS

There are so many virtual care and remote on-call doctors available. While this isn't the first idea that comes to mind if you've hurt yourself, it's a great way to get medical attention immediately if you're unsure if your insurance will cover you, or you are in a different state than your normal doctor. An increasing number of medical services are being offered remotely as the system adapts to changing current events.

HOW TO DEAL WITH YOUR PARTNER

How to coexist on the road is so incredibly specific to each individual partnership. We have many systems in place that help us to deal with each others' idiosyncrasies and the deeper issues between the two of us. No matter who the partner (or if you're working through your own emotions alone), here are some tips that have helped us:

- Purposefully take time apart, or take time specifically for yourself. One person can hike or bike while the other stays back and reads. One can take the left trail while the other goes right. Set up specific time to be apart and enjoy it with just yourself.

- Put dedicated energy into relationships outside of your partner, or in your relationships outside of van life. Van life can be very isolating. Set aside valuable time to talk to a friend on the phone, write a letter to a family member, or physically meet up with someone. Putting a focus on other connections can do incredible things for your partnership as well as your mental health. There is no way your partner can fulfill every emotional need you have, so spread the love to friends and family.

- Have "plan days" and "execution days." Having to make constant decisions throughout a week or month puts a real strain on your mental load (your constantly running to-do list). Concentrate planning into a day or two and then executing over the next few weeks to take the pressure off the question "where do we go next?"

- Even though you're with your partner every hour of every day (most of the time), you still have to *date* them. Go out of your way to do small kind acts, compliment, or express appreciation. This also applies to those traveling alone—date yourself! Buy some chocolate, watch a funny movie—you're worth it.

- You are a team! This is exponentially reinforced during van life. When you get a flat in the middle of nowhere, one partner can't just walk away and sleep at a friend's house. You both have to figure out the next steps together. Face crises as a team, there is no point in wasting energy battling with each other when there are bigger things to handle. As an individual, the disasters will exercise your mental fortitude. You can do this.

ONLINE CAREER COUNSELING

How to make money on the road can be a huge stressor, and having someone guide you on your career journey can be a huge help. There are so many remote and online services ready to help you find out the best way for you to pay the bills and fund your adventures.

HOBBIES

The time at camp when the sunset stretches through the sky is beautiful, but it can also be a time when loneliness creeps up. We always make exceptions for hobbies when weighing an object's use to the space it takes up. You can only read for so many hours in the day. Explore new crafts and hobbies in your no-service time. This is also a great time

to practice instruments—guitar, ukulele, travel didgeridoo, harmonica, there are so many options.

ENTERTAINMENT

There are many streaming services that allow you to download shows for offline viewing. Utilize Redbox and other movie rental services. Watching a good flick with the crickets singing in the background can remind you of how great van life can be.

STAY CONNECTED

Remember to check in with your core group often and visit when possible. New road friends are genuine and uplifting, but being able to say "Remember when . . ." is soothing to the soul.

chapter 10 BRING YOUR PET ALONG FOR THE RIDE

THERE ARE SO MANY DIFFERENT TYPES OF HUMANS and relationship combinations that can cohabitate in a van. Families, couples, friends, solo, or surrounded by a community along the way. All of these combinations have one thing in common: There's usually room left over for furry friends! There are long lists of pros and cons when adding a non-humanoid adventure buddy. Ultimately, it's up to you if you think your animal is up for the new lifestyle.

Most pets are highly adaptable, and many enjoy the freedom of the great outdoors just as much as their brave caretakers. We personally travel with our adventure dog, Henry, who has grown accustomed to free rein at campsites, new smells every night, dog friends all over the country, and attention from almost every human that passes by.

The positive aspects of traveling with a pet are abundant. Here are a few of them:

- Added companionship
- A feeling of safety
- A furry pillow when you're having a hard day
- Extra reasons to exercise
- A calming presence
- Endless love

The cons of having an animal with you on the road get more complicated. Animals of all types need a lot of care, and it's harder to provide consistent routine care when living nomadically. Here are some issues you may run into with bringing your pet on the road:

- Not being able to leave your animal in the car during the summer months while you run errands or explore areas where pets aren't allowed

CATE & CHAD BATTLES

CATE AND CHAD HAD BEEN PLANNING their great adventure after raising kids and running a business in Asheville, North Carolina. Once the kids were on their own, they sold the house, hit the road, and planned to eventually pick a new home out west.

VEHICLE + WHY
2011 GMC Envoy pulling an Airstream—it's decent with gas and comfortable for our goat.

CONNECT
@argosyodyssey

TIME ON THE ROAD
Full-time, 4 years

PETS ON THE ROAD
Pets provide constant entertainment, especially Frankie the goat! There are also a fair number of caveats to traveling with pets—we make it work though, and we find plenty of places the three of us can explore on BLM and national forest land. Expect to not be able to do all the things you had hoped to unless you have a partner that can take turns with you. Take the animals on a scenic drive and get pictures at the overlooks, then find a place outside of the national park boundaries to hike—oftentimes, they are just as beautiful.

- Creating and maintaining a consistent feeding and exercise schedule
- Added dirt and wear and tear inside your vehicle
- An animal takes up extra space in an already small environment (although we haven't run into a single van lifer who has complained about this)
- Having to use different vets if issues arise
- The added cost of food and care

The cons of having your animal with you seem more concrete and serious. But that doesn't mean the cons outweigh the pros—we think it's quite the opposite.

Here are a few helpful hints and tips to take into consideration as you build your van life dreams and intentions. We have a dog with us on the road, so most of the tips center around canines but can apply to all types of animals. We know plenty of van lifers with cats and other types of pets who really enjoy the company.

HOW TO START

Including an animal in your daily tasks can be overwhelming if you're still trying to figure out how to take care of yourself. If you're feeling nervous, have a friend take care of your animal for a few weeks while you get your tires under you. This is one possible way to see if having a pet on the road will work out for you, or if it is best to find other arrangements for them while you're traveling.

Serious consideration should go into the sacrifices you will have to make surrounding how you spend your time. Depending on the time of year, leaving your furry friend in the car just isn't an option. Sometimes, this means skipping an exciting outdoor activity because your pet isn't allowed. Sometimes it means going out of your way to find an animal-friendly campsite. For most devoted pet owners, this is already second nature.

FOOD AND WATER

Keep a special container for your animal's food and water. Use containers that are water-proof and spill-proof (barring human error, and we have a lot of errors). The first reason this is helpful is so their food doesn't get wet and you don't have to dump out the water every time you move to a new location.

Giving your pet enough opportunities to eat and drink might mean taking more time at gas station stops, finding places to put their bowls at friends' houses, and closing the food and water each evening so critters don't get into it.

LEEANN JUDAY

LEEANN MOVED INTO A VAN to pursue a travel-based lifestyle. The van acted as a home while she paid off land and home construction costs. Van life also allowed the time and space for more naps and breaks, which she requires due to Asperger's overload.

VEHICLE + WHY
1996 Ford Work Van—this will be my first complete build-out.

CONNECT
@AspieOnTheRoad

TIME ON THE ROAD
Full-time, 7 years

PETS ON THE ROAD
Living with Aya (a giant woolly malamute) in the van can present some challenges since she is most comfortable in a colder alpine climate. I travel with the weather to accommodate her. She's just as needy in a house. Sometimes it's easier to handle her needs on the road simply because taking care of a home takes a lot of time and effort. Plan your day around your pet, not the other way around.

LEEANN JUDAY

EXERCISE

On long travel days, our floof ball is just as antsy as we are in the van. Gas stations usually have a grass plot to stretch both human and dog legs. Do a walkover first to check for broken glass and anything else dangerous your pet may encounter. Use a glow-in-the-dark tennis ball to play fetch if you get to camp after dark.

On adventure days our dog tires himself out and puts himself to bed early. These are the days that make #vandog travel so rewarding. When we hike he is often off-leash if the regulations allow it. We've found our dog gets far more exercise living in a van compared to sticks and bricks. Instead of one or two long walks a day, he is constantly on the move with us.

"YOUR DOG BEHAVES SO WELL!"

Having a well-behaved pet with you makes the difference between burden and adventure buddy. We spent hours and hours with our dog when he was a puppy, training him after our workday. We're still training him. We work on behavior every day so we can

SYDNEY FERBRACHE

SYDNEY WAS GROWING INCREASINGLY UNHAPPY while working seventy hours a week in the restaurant industry and knew something needed to change. Now she lives full-time in a van with her two dogs, Ella and Pearl. Sydney acts as a resource for others looking for similar freedom by hosting her own podcast called *My Solo Road*, building a website that details all the logistics, and sharing daily through social media platforms.

SYDNEY FERBRACHE

VEHICLE + WHY:
2017 Ford Transit High Roof—I passionately hate Sprinters, I don't care for the way Pro-Masters look, and I'm tall so I needed one of those three.

CONNECT
@divineontheroad @mysoloroad

TIME ON THE ROAD
Full-time, 3 years

PETS ON THE ROAD
Just learn to cater to your animal. You can't do those three hikes . . . okay, you can probably do a hundred other ones. That restaurant doesn't allow dogs? Go to one that does! Your animals have to be at the top of your mind all the time, which sounds exhausting—but they are my favorite part of van life so it doesn't bother me one bit. I could not imagine being entirely alone for this. They bring me companionship while still getting to "find myself" outside of an actual relationship.

The best piece of advice I can give is to train them off-leash. I wouldn't get any work done if I couldn't have my dogs off-leash without worrying about them. I can park at a campsite with all my doors open. I can be on my bed and they're outside. Because they are so low maintenance, I can do what I want all day and they can walk/run around as much as they need to.

continue bringing him along for the ride. We used a softer version of the Koehler Method. In essence, you and your dog are a pack of two and the human is the lead dog at all times.

DIRT IN YOUR HOME

If you're choosing to live in a van, then you've already chosen to live a life among the dirt. Your bed will get dirty, your floor will be a mess, and your pets will love it. Shake everything out, bring a broom and dustpan, and embrace the dirt. It's like sleeping in a bed of sand, but the sand is dried mud (or actual sand depending on where you're camping). Laundry opportunities are few and far between, but wash whatever you can, whenever possible. Using pet brushes and having a dedicated "animal towel" for wiping down pets before they get back in the van can help, but nothing will stop the small bits and pieces of outside from taking up residence in your home.

PROTIP

You'll be spending a lot of time driving, and statistically, driving is a fairly dangerous thing to do. Luckily, your rig has seat belts! It is in your furry friends' best interest to be restrained as well. There are many options out there in terms of retrofitting pet-restraint systems. Consider giving your BFF a seat belt as well!

HEALTH AND LEAVING YOUR ANIMAL UNATTENDED IN YOUR VEHICLE

Health is our number-one concern when traveling with our pet. Tick checks, shots, and rest after an injury are all regular occurrences. Our pup has become graceful in the outdoors, and it's a pleasure to watch him enjoy being outside as much as we do. But that doesn't mean he comes home clean and injury-free every evening. His paws get cut up, he gets ticks under his coat, and he is exposed to a lot of weird bacteria in lakes and

streams. Give your best friend the rest they need, check them for ticks every night (also yourselves), and get them to the vet for a checkup whenever you're near.

On the off-chance something happens while you are far from your home veterinarian, have that vet communicate records to the one you visit in the current town, and carry a hard copy. Alternatively, you can bring your animal to a veterinarian that's located in a chain pet store like PetSmart or Petco.

Leaving your pet in the van in warmer temperatures can be dangerous. It can also be unavoidable. It gets treacherous very quickly when the van starts to heat up. If it is unavoidable, use fans, leave water, put up window covers, and always park in the shade to keep temperatures in the van down.

One of the benefits of having a partner is being able to divide and conquer. One can go into a store while the other stays in the van with your pet to make sure it stays at a good temperature. This may not be possible for solo van lifers, so the fan and window shades are your best bet. You can also purchase an inexpensive thermometer with Bluetooth so you will always know exactly how hot it is in your van. As a general rule, if you are in doubt, never leave them alone in warmer temperatures.

There are plenty of places your pets won't be allowed throughout the country. One of the most challenging is national parks. In most national parks, dogs are allowed in campgrounds and on paved trails, but that's it. This is for good reason! Besides being a threat to native wildlife, dog poop in the wilderness can introduce compounds that wouldn't have been there without the presence of a domesticated dog, which can upset the balance of that system. There are usually vast stretches of public land sitting right outside the gates of national parks where dogs are allowed. At some parks, we have found the free public lands are closer to the trails we want to explore than the campgrounds inside the park.

Here are suggestions for exploring national parks safely with a pet:

- Leave your animal with a trusted sitter, friend, or family member. This can be hard to arrange a drop off and pick up when you want to leave before sunrise or camp for a few days. It can also be expensive. Rover.com is a good resource for finding pet-sitters outside the park entrances. There are sacrifices you have to make in order to live on the road with your pet, and extra drive time is one of them.
- Only go on trails and viewpoints where animals are allowed. Keep them leashed, close by, and pick up any waste along the way.

PET-FRIENDLY NATIONAL PARKS

BLACK CANYON OF THE GUNNISON: Pets walk on roads, in campgrounds, to the overlooks, and are allowed on the Cedar Point Nature Trail, North Rim Chasm View Nature Trail, and Rim Rock Trail.

GRAND CANYON NATIONAL PARK: Thirteen miles of the South Rim Trail are accessible with your pet. There are also plenty of overlooks that allow animals on a leash.

GREAT SAND DUNES NATIONAL PARK: Pets are welcome up to the top of the first tall ridge of dunes, between High Dune and the Castle Creek Picnic Area, and throughout the adjoining Great Sand Dunes National Preserve.

SHENANDOAH NATIONAL PARK: There are more than five hundred miles of trails in this park and only twenty miles are off-limits to pets (due to climbing obstructions). The hike to the top of Turk Mountain is perfect for dogs and has a great view at the end.

CONGAREE NATIONAL PARK: Pets are allowed on all trails, including the boardwalk, as well as in the campgrounds.

EXTRAS

Some of the items on our packing list for pets are obvious so we'll just address a few of the items below that might not be as self-explanatory. You know your pet better than

anyone so you can adapt this list as you see fit. For a complete packing list for your animal, see chapter 14.

- A reflective vest for traveling in hunting areas
- LED glow collar
- Evaporative cooling vest for desert and high-temperature travel
- Pet trimmer and a pair of scissors
- Nail clippers
- A dedicated pet towel

PROTIP

Challenges are often surprises—like when your dog rolls in something and you have to wash them, or they eat something that upsets their stomach and have an accident in the van. Be sure they have a way to stay cool if staying in the van for a long period of time, and be aware of (and prepared for) their needs to explore, jump in the water, lay in your bed, or go to the bathroom when you just want to get there already! **—RANDI & STEVE HITCHCOCK**

EXPLORING
+ BEYOND

chapter 11 VAN LIFE IN THE NATIONAL PARKS

THE NATIONAL PARK SERVICE LOOKS AFTER SIXTY-TWO PARKS in the United States, each protected by their own act of Congress. These protected lands offer vast playgrounds for travel, exploration, and outdoor adventure. National parks are also often very van friendly, with amenities like free or cheap camping, passable entry roads, and travel-supporting businesses in surrounding towns. National parks have a few little things that van lifers never take for granted. They usually have free water at the visitor centers and offer recycling and trash services. Some campgrounds within the parks even have places to recycle empty fuel canisters.

National park destinations are a great way to structure a trip, summer, or year. Of course, there is land that is just as beautiful right outside these parks—but the parks are a wonder to behold and definitely a high priority for a lot of van lifers.

The national parks are scattered throughout the United States. A total of twenty-nine states harbor homes for these protected lands. Some of the parks, like the three that span from Utah to Arizona, are all related. Bryce Canyon National Park, located at over eight thousand feet, is connected via fault lines through Escalante with Zion National Park, which leads down to Grand Canyon National Park at a little over two thousand feet. Visiting all three in succession gives you a feeling of the deep history of the land, both ancestrally and geologically, over thousands of millions of years.

Out of respect for the original custodians of these beautiful and enchanting park lands, indigenous nations are indicated within each park description below. We recognize that these lands are still under dispute. If you find peace and fulfillment from the beauty of these lands, please consider donating to the tribes themselves or to organizations helping to promote awareness of this topic. Educate yourself on the history and current situation of indigenous peoples.

What follows is a highlight reel of the parks, organized regionally, with essential camping, hiking, and recreational information to kickstart the adventure. **Please note:** The free campsites mentioned here were open and legal at the time of this writing. Please check with the local ranger district to get the most accurate and up-to-date camping information. Always have a backup plan in case a site is closed. It's a great idea to plan on getting to camp with plenty of light left in the day, so if something isn't available there is time to find a safe spot before the sun sets.

NORTHEAST

THE NEW RIVER GORGE NATIONAL PARK AND PRESERVE, WEST VIRGINIA

NATIVE LANDS: S'atsoyaha (Yuchi), Tutelo, Moneton

The New River Gorge draws outdoor enthusiasts from across the world. Here you'll find the wild and scenic New River situated in a massive gorge that was cut by the elements. This area offers world-class rock climbing and deep-water soloing, seemingly endless whitewater opportunities, and once a year on Bridge Day, legal base jumping off the New River Gorge Bridge. The New River Gorge National Park and Preserve area only offers free, primitive camping.

FREE PLACE TO CAMP IN THE PARK: Glade Creek Campground
GPS: N37.854561' / W81.059532'
Right on the New River, this primitive campground has bathrooms and beachside campsites.

Suggested Hike
ENDLESS WALL TRAIL
2.3 miles, easy, 288 feet elevation gain

This hike is peaceful and provides panoramic views of the New River almost one thousand feet below. Look closely to spot rock climbers enjoying the sandstone walls that line the gorge below.

Other Recreational Opportunities

Climbers come from all over the world to take advantage of over 1,600 rock-climbing routes in the area. The gorge is rimmed with sandstone cliffs, but the climbing opportunities don't stop there. Just a short drive away, assuming the lake is at the right level, you can deep-water solo (climb on the rocks and jump into the water below) at Summersville Lake. We recommend stopping in Fayetteville, West Virginia, and snagging a guidebook for the area. There are so many routes, some bolted (set up for sport climbing), some not, that without a guidebook it's really hard to know what you're getting yourself into.

This area is also known for whitewater rafting. Sure, you can raft the New River for something more mellow, but if you come when the Army Corps of Engineers stages a dam release on the Gauley River, things get really spicy (Class V).

SHENANDOAH NATIONAL PARK, VIRGINIA

NATIVE LANDS: Manahoac

Interstate 81 runs like a spine down the west side of Virginia, with ample access to scenic van camping, interesting trails (many along the Appalachian Trail system), the northern section of the beautiful 469-mile Blue Ridge Parkway, and Shenandoah National Park.

FREE PLACE TO CAMP CLOSE TO THE PARK: Braley Pond Dispersed Campground

GPS: N38.28611' / W79.301941'

~1 hour to South Entrance of Shenandoah National Park

Multiple sites featuring a lake and hiking trails.

LOW-COST CAMPING INSIDE THE PARK: Mathews Arm, Big Meadows, and Loft Mountain

$15 to $20 per night

Mathews Arm: N38.760348' / W78.297749'

Big Meadows: N38.528020' / W78.438930'

Loft Mountain: N38.247640' / W78.667998'

No hookups, but potable water and dump stations are available.

Suggested Hikes
OLD RAG: Oldy, goody, great view
9.2-mile loop, strenuous, 2,380 feet elevation gain
This is a popular one, and for good reason. Arrive early (actually early) and be ready to spend at least a few hours climbing to the summit. The views of the sweeping Blue Ridge Mountains are worth it, especially if you actually left early and the morning light is still highlighting the rolling forests.
TURK MOUNTAIN: Short but with great reward
2.2 miles out and back, moderate, 690 feet elevation gain
This hike is a favorite because dogs are allowed on leash, and the top-out point is great for a picnic (if you're willing to balance your sandwich on a rock).

SOUTHEAST

CONGAREE NATIONAL PARK, SOUTH CAROLINA
NATIVE LANDS: Congaree, Cherokee, East
This isn't the easiest national park to camp by, but it's worth it. Say hello to the snakes, alligators, and massive spiders while you explore the mystical swamp.
FREE PLACE TO CAMP CLOSE TO THE PARK: Halfway Creek Trail Camp
GPS: N33.056686' / W79.696588'
~2 hours from Harry Hampton Visitor Center, Congaree National Park. While this is far from the park, it's close to the South Carolina beaches!
LOW-COST CAMPING OUTSIDE THE PARK: While there are only walk-in campsites available (which you must reserve ahead of time and might be fun for a night out of the van), there are two state parks within forty-five minutes of the Congaree National Park visitor center. If Santee State Park is full, check out Poinsett State Park. Both have 50-amp service, dump stations, and sites with electricity and water.
Santee State Park, $20 to $44 per night
GPS: N33.551293' / W80.501245'
Reservations must be made two nights in advance.

Suggested Hike
BOARDWALK LOOP TRAIL: Slippery walkway and swamp monsters
2.4 miles, easy, 76 feet elevation gain
This ADA-accessible, family-friendly walk is still full of thrills. Expect a menagerie of animals as you balance your way along the elevated boardwalk.

Other Recreational Opportunities
For a truly unique experience, spend some time camping and recreating around Lake Marion, South Carolina's largest lake. If you plan on traveling with watercraft, put in at the

Sparkleberry Landing. You'll instantly find yourself feeling like you're exploring another planet. The Sparkleberry Swamp is situated at the headwaters of Lake Marion. Navigating through the beautiful cypress and tupelo trees draped in Spanish moss is an incredible experience. If you decide to check out the swamp, it's advisable to carry a GPS so you can retrace your route. Some of the trees have painted markings on them to show you a safe passage, however it's extremely easy to get lost once you enter the trees. Be cautious of alligators (keep your smaller pets secure), and never feed the wildlife.

GREAT SMOKY MOUNTAINS NATIONAL PARK, NORTH CAROLINA AND TENNESSEE

NATIVE LANDS: Cherokee, East, S'atsoyaha (Yuchi)

There's something magical about these rolling blue and green hills with light fog resting silently in the valleys. Little did we know the "smoke" is actually VOCs (volatile organic compounds, the same thing you smell when close to a pine tree) released from the vegetation resting in between the undulating skylines creating vapor—fog. Come early in the morning and see it for yourself, then continue the day fully relaxed.

FREE PLACE TO CAMP CLOSE TO THE PARK: Due to the development and private land surrounding the park, finding free camping is slightly more challenging than in some of the other national parks.

Panther Creek FDR #2604B

GPS: N35.370841' / W83.627873'

~40 minutes to Oconaluftee Visitor Center

This is a free dispersed camping area in Nantahala National Forest.

Santeetlah Lake
GPS: N35.367268' / W83.853607'
~1 hour to Oconaluftee Visitor Center
If you don't mind adding twenty minutes to your drive, you can camp for free on the water at Santeetlah Lake.
LOW-COST CAMPING INSIDE THE PARK: Abrams Creek Campground, $17.50
GPS: N35.611170' / W83.933703'
No hookups, but great accessibility to the hikes in the park.

Suggested Hikes
RAINBOW FALLS TRAIL: Scamper up through the woods for a refreshing waterfall payoff.
5.5 miles, strenuous (deceivingly so), 1,653 feet elevation gain
Up and up and up on this one. While the waterfall might not be the most spectacular, the misty East Coast forests, twinkling streams, and rock outcroppings are fit for a fairy. Head past the waterfalls (if you have the energy) for a bonus view. Keep an eye out for bears in springtime and slugs in the summer.
CHARLIES BUNION VIA APPALACHIAN TRAIL: A taste of the AT
8.6 miles, strenuous, 1,981 feet elevation gain
Jump on this trail for a little taste of what all the grungy hikers experience along their journey from Georgia to Maine. Make it all the way and get rewarded with a classic Blue Ridge scene—layers of rounded mountains viewed from Charlies Bunion, ahem, a rock outcropping.

Other Recreational Opportunities
One of our favorite things to do in this area of the country is mountain biking. From the park, you are less than a two-hour drive from the mountain-biking mecca Brevard, North Carolina. From town you can bike straight into Pisgah National Forest and never stop riding.

This area is also known for its whitewater rafting. While the Pigeon River is closest to the most popular side of the park, you can also raft the Nantahala, Nolichucky, and French Broad Rivers not too far away.

PROTIP

For me, happiness on the road is highly dependent on weather, especially because my goal is to spend as much time outdoors as possible. In the East you can't park wherever you want and public land and neighborly goodwill is scarce. I spent three long, rainy weeks in New Hampshire because I had an itinerary, but I should have ditched the East Coast ASAP and headed west. **—CONNIE**

MIDWEST

BADLANDS NATIONAL PARK, SOUTH DAKOTA

NATIVE LANDS: Cheyenne, Mnicoujou, Očeti Šakówiŋ

If your trip takes you through North Dakota, Badlands National Park is a must-see. It's home to alien-like rock formations and expansive views. Don't be fooled by the northern location, it will still be aggressively hot in the summertime. Plan to come in spring or fall for comfortable temperatures.

FREE PLACE TO CAMP CLOSE TO THE PARK: Sage Creek Campground

This is a *free* campground *in* the national park, how great is that?! It is first-come, first-served, with a limit of eighteen feet for vehicle length. Fourteen-day limit. Watch for buffalo when heading to the pit toilets.
GPS: N43.894967' / W102.413442'

LOW-COST CAMPING INSIDE THE PARK: Cedar Pass Campground $22 to $37 per night depending on the number of people and hookups.
Open for summer months, check the NPS site for exact dates.
Dump station available for $1. Cold running water, flush toilets.
GPS: N43.746181' / W101.948326'

Other Recreational Opportunities

This is mainly a driving national park; hiking's not the attraction. There are many overlooks and stopping points along the road that runs through it. We highly suggest renting or bringing bicycles and making a day of riding the road. It's a great way to take in the scenery and experience the park from a different perspective.

One of the true gems in this part of South Dakota is the Black Hills. Visit Custer State Park for epic views and some of the best rock climbing in the country. Here and in the surrounding area, you'll find nearly six hundred trad and sport routes. After you're done climbing, be sure to cool off by swimming in Sylvan Lake.

WIND CAVE NATIONAL PARK, SOUTH DAKOTA

NATIVE LANDS: Očeti Šakówiŋ, Cheyenne

There are quite a number of national parks meant to preserve caves: Carlsbad Caverns, Mammoth Cave, and Jewel Cave to name a few. Wind Cave is an exciting visit because you can pair it with other features in the area. It's a great choice for when the weather isn't cooperating or you want a break from the heat of the summer.

FREE PLACE TO CAMP CLOSE TO THE PARK: Big Valley
GPS: N43.724153' / W103.539858'
~30 minutes to Wind Cave National Park Visitor Center
A valley with a stream and plenty of places to park. Close to Wind Cave National Park and Custer State Park.
LOW-COST CAMPING INSIDE THE PARK: Elk Mountain Campground, $9 to $18 per night
Water and flush toilets accessible for half the year.
GPS: N43.565264' / W103.489396'

Suggested Hike

BLACK ELK PEAK SOUTH DAKOTA HIGHPOINT TRAIL IN CUSTER STATE PARK

This hike is actually outside of Wind Cave National Park (because WCNP is mostly underground).
7.6 miles, 1,551 feet elevation gain
Welcome to the highest peak east of the Rockies! Make your way up to Black Elk Peak and relax at the abandoned fire tower at the top. Enjoy the weird rock spires and views along the way.

Other Recreational Opportunities

The only way to experience this weird cave is by taking a tour. Don't worry, they aren't expensive ($10–$12) and run often! Prepare for stairs, spooky cave formations, and an explanation of why it's called the "Wind Cave." Go in the morning or evening to avoid crowds during the summer.

WEST

YELLOWSTONE NATIONAL PARK, IDAHO, MONTANA, AND WYOMING

NATIVE LANDS: Apsaalooké (Crow), Cheyenne, Shoshone-Bannock
Yellowstone is so large, beautiful, and full of wildlife, it's hard to narrow it down to a few campsites and hikes. If you're planning a visit or a drive-through on a road trip, cushion a few extra days to see what this magical place has to offer.
Please note: Yellowstone National Park is home to a lively grizzly bear population, and food storage is required for camping in or near the park. It is best to carry bear spray when recreating in this area. Many camping areas around Yellowstone only allow camping in hard-sided vehicles.
FREE PLACE TO CAMP CLOSE TO THE PARK: National Forest Road 3243
GPS: N45.070611' / W110.680043'
~45 minutes to the Albright Visitor Center (this is not the main visitor center, this is the north entrance)

May be crowded, but what isn't around Yellowstone? This is a camp spot on the north entrance, but there are also options for staying on public land on the east and west sides.
LOW-COST CAMPING INSIDE THE PARK: This is one of the most popular national parks in the country (and our nation's first!), and because of that, it is often crowded. There are twelve campgrounds with over two thousand sites. Five sites take reservations and all the others are first-come, first-served. Many have all the amenities you would need in a full-hookup site. You can find any information you'd need about camping in the park on the park's website.

Mammoth Campground, $20 per night
85 sites; first-come, first-served; flush toilets
GPS: N44.976171' / W110.693831'

Suggested Hike

GRAND PRISMATIC HOT SPRING: And you thought rainbows were just for the sky.
1.2 miles, easy, 105 feet elevation gain
There are hundreds of geysers in Yellowstone National Park and more than ten thousand hydrothermal features. Pick a few to see—Old Faithful erupts every 35 to 120 minutes, and our personal favorite is Puff 'n Stuff (but only for the name). On the list should be Grand Prismatic, an otherworldly hot spring that seems to bleed the rainbow.

Other Recreational Opportunities

BOILING RIVER SOAK: Feel the hot springs instead of looking at them.
1.2 miles, easy, 75 feet elevation gain
The Boiling River flows into the Gardner River near the north entrance to the park. There are separate pools, but everything is built by moving rocks from place to place, so don't expect temperature regulation. The only facilities are a pit toilet at the parking lot. Yellowstone's Lamar Valley is home to abundant wildlife including bison, wolves, grizzly bears, and black bears. If you make it to the Lamar Valley for sunset, and more importantly sunrise, this area of the park is excellent for wildlife viewing.

YOSEMITE NATIONAL PARK, CALIFORNIA

NATIVE LANDS: Me-Wuk (Southern and Central Sierra Miwok)
Iconic doesn't begin to describe Yosemite. From watching climbers on the Dawn Wall to seeing the towering monoliths light up at sunset from Tunnel View lookout point, Yosemite is breathtaking all day long. Take a few days to soak it all in, and give yourself a chance to get permits for the more popular hikes.
FREE PLACE TO CAMP CLOSE TO THE PARK: Saddlebag Lake parking lot
Lee Vining, California
GPS: N37.96568' / W119.27109'
~25 minutes to Tuolumne Meadows Visitor Center
~2 hours to Yosemite Valley Visitor Center
This site is near the east entrance to Yosemite National Park. There are few pull-offs on your way up if you see something that piques your interest. Be warned—it's chilly up at 10,125 feet. It's a great jumping-off point for exploring along Tiaga Road, which runs directly through the park.
LOW-COST CAMPING INSIDE THE PARK: If you're going to explore the heart of Yosemite National Park, Yosemite Valley, we suggest reserving a camping spot well in advance. They've made it pretty hard to find a free van spot nearby, so if you want to be there for a few days to explore, you'll want an official camp spot inside the park. There are thirteen campgrounds, and seven of those take reservations. Reserve early. First-come, first-served campsites fill up quickly as well, usually by noon or earlier. It's cutthroat camping in Yosemite Valley!

Pines Campground, $26/night
Dump station available at the entrance to Upper Pines, no hookups
GPS: N37.739368' / W119.565487'

Suggested Hikes

HALF DOME TRAIL: Cables and elevation, oh my!
14.8 miles, strenuous, 5,164 feet elevation gain

PROTIP

Apply for a backcountry permit that includes Half Dome, or apply for a first-come,
first-served wilderness permit beginning 11 a.m. one day before your backpacking
trip.

PROTIP

Tuolumne Meadows is my favorite patch of earth. I must have a deep affinity for granite domes. The logistics aren't easy, but there's nothing like having the entire Sierra at your fingertips and nowhere else in the world to be. **—CONNIE**

This hike is for the dedicated. Expect to leave before sunrise and hike for ten to twelve hours. We would not attempt this hike without a summer of training beforehand. There is a permit system for this hike. At the time of this writing, you could put your name in the pre-season lottery or attempt to grab a permit in the daily lottery. The daily permits are applied for two days in advance.

GLACIER POINT TRAIL: Fast track to sweeping views

0.6 mile, easy, 236 feet elevation gain

The road to this hike is a beautiful drive leading you up and out of Yosemite Valley. It's a quick jump out of the car for a full view of the valley below. Upper and Lower Yosemite Falls, Clouds Rest, and Half Dome are all there, standing proud and tall. The road is closed in winter, but that's just an excuse to cross-country ski or snowshoe your way to the viewpoint. You can even book a night at Glacier Point Ski Hut complete with bunk beds and a cozy wood fire.

REDWOOD NATIONAL AND STATE PARKS, CALIFORNIA

NATIVE LANDS: Tolowa Dee-ni', Yurok, Wiyot, Mattole, Tsnungwe, Hoopa

Seeing a redwood tree is akin to going back in time. These behemoths were around before Julius Caesar spoke his last words. If you weren't a tree hugger before, enter with arms wide open. While driving through these groves is impressive, getting out and walking among these giants will really give you a new perspective.

The Redwood National and State Parks are a patchwork of land that is now protected from logging and other special interests after a long and difficult fight. Most of the land was donated to the State of California to create three state parks. It wasn't until 1968 that Congress acted to protect an additional 58,000 acres of land surrounding the parks to create Redwood National Park. For this reason, this park is a little different than many national parks because there isn't just one destination that is considered "the park."

FREE PLACE TO CAMP CLOSE TO THE PARK: Camping for free near the coast in California is notoriously challenging. It's such a popular area that it is illegal to camp in most places outside of established campgrounds. While some of the popular camping apps show free places to camp, they usually get closed within a few days. We recommend reserving a spot in one of the many campgrounds inside the park.

LOW-COST CAMPING INSIDE THE PARK: All of the campgrounds within Redwood State and National Parks cost $35 for a van-sized spot and require an $8 reservation fee. It's also important to note that camping in this area is highly competitive and you should reserve your spot well in advance. That being said, the campgrounds are really nice and you have the option to sleep beneath redwoods or even camp on the beach.

Suggested Hikes
JAMES IRVINE TRAIL: Considered one of the best hikes in the entire park system
10.7 miles, moderate, 1,604 feet elevation gain
This lightly trafficked hike will make you feel like you're in another world. This journey might be 10.7 miles long, but the natural beauty will have you forgetting about the distance once you're on the trail. Located inside Prairie Creek State Park, this trail wanders through old-growth redwoods down to the beach.
LADY BIRD JOHNSON GROVE: A short hike through a stunning old-growth redwood grove
1.4 miles, easy, 75 feet elevation gain
This is one of the most popular hikes in the Redwood State and National Parks system. It provides easy access to some truly spectacular trees. Due to the location of this hike, the forest is often filled with fog, making a walk in the forest feel like a dream.

Other Recreational Opportunities
Go to the beach, obviously.

SOUTHWEST

CANYONLANDS NATIONAL PARK, UTAH
NATIVE LANDS: Núu-agha-tʉvʉ-pʉ (Ute), Pueblos
Everyone heads straight to Arches National Park, but we are here to tell you Canyonlands should be top of the list in the Moab area. This park is only a little farther to drive, has half the people, and offers incredible desert sites. You can also check out Dead Horse Point State Park for dog-friendly options with exceptional canyon views.
FREE PLACE TO CAMP CLOSE TO THE PARK: Hamburger Rock, Lock Hart Road
~15 minutes from Needles District Visitor Center
~2 hours from Island in the Sky Visitor Center
GPS: N38.199499' / W109.671155'
This spot is just past Hamburger Rock campground ($15) and surrounded by massive rock formations. It's close to the Needles Entrance of the park. There are many other free campsites around this area.
LOW-COST CAMPING INSIDE THE PARK: Island in the Sky, Willow Flat Campground, $15 per night, first-come, first-served
Toilet, picnic table, and fire ring; no hookups or water
GPS: N38.382371' / W109.888627'

Suggested Hikes
CHESLER PARK TO JOINT TRAIL TO DRUID ARCH LOOP: The best of Needles district
15 miles, strenuous, 2,539 feet elevation gain

This loop takes you out and around Chesler Park, through the Joint Trail (with a super-fun slot canyon section), and finishes with a side trip to Druid Arch if you're feeling up for it (which if you left early enough and packed enough snacks, we highly recommend). We suggest doing this loop counterclockwise. Always check the weather beforehand, pack more water than you expect you'll need, and keep an eye out for aliens . . . or are those just the rock formations?

SYNCLINE LOOP (lollipop): A dip into the mysterious Upheaval Crater
8.3 miles, strenuous, 1,300 feet elevation gain
Not for the faint of heart or legs. This wonderful hike will take you down and around the Upheaval Crater, a huge dome area theorized to be created by a meteorite (or a salt dome, another theory). We suggest proceeding clockwise around this loop, saving the rock scrambling and route finding for uphill about halfway through the hike. If you have the time, take a peek into the crater. And if you have even more time, spend the night. Just remember to grab a backcountry permit.

Other Recreational Opportunities

Thousands of miles of public lands stretch for as far as the eye can see outside Canyonlands. You can rock climb the famous sandstone cracks and towers. You can head into Moab and rent an off-road vehicle to do some rock crawling in the desert. Then of course there's the slick rock that makes for incredible mountain biking. When you're finished adventuring you can head just north of town and cool off in the Colorado River.

GRAND CANYON NATIONAL PARK, ARIZONA

NATIVE LANDS: Hopi, Hualapai, Havasupai, Pueblos, Southern Paiute

This national park is a bucket-list topper. Catch an overlook at sunrise or sunset and you will be changed forever. Score a backcountry permit and immerse yourself in the magic of the canyon.

FREE PLACE TO CAMP CLOSE TO THE PARK: Kaibab National Forest campground
GPS: N35.963141' / W111.965377'
~20 minutes to the Grand Canyon Visitor Center
A no-frills area where you are close enough to the park to catch sunset and sunrise over the canyon.

LOW-COST CAMPING INSIDE THE PARK: Mather Campground, $18 per night
No hookups (hookups only available at Trailer Village adjacent to Mather Campground), close to the main village, coffee bar within walking distance.
GPS: N36.051037' / W112.121226'

Suggested Hikes

RIM-TO-RIM: See GCNP from all angles.
24 miles one-way, strenuous, 5,150 feet elevation gain
This grueling, and we mean *grueling*, hike gets you views of the canyon from all sides. With an early morning start (before the sun is up) expect to be hiking all day, but also experience the magic of the canyon, all day. Most hikers take a shuttle to the north side early in the morning and hike back toward their vehicle parked on the south side. If you plan months ahead, you can reserve a spot at Bright Angel Campground at the bottom of the canyon. Bring all the water you can carry, and then bring an extra bottle. Don't attempt this hike in the heat of midsummer.

RIM TRAIL: 13 miles of paved walkway with expansive views
13 miles one-way, easy, varied elevation gain
Pick a few miles to experience, walk the whole thing, or time the bus schedule correctly and get a ride back to your vehicle. Dogs are allowed on leash, and markers show you how far you've traveled both physically and in years spanning back through the canyon's creation. Head toward Grandeur Point for sunset or Shoshone Point for sunrise.

ZION NATIONAL PARK, UTAH

NATIVE LANDS: Southern Paiute, Pueblos, Núu-agha-tuvu-pu (Ute)
We were sure Zion was all hype and no delivery before we visited. But then it blew us out of the canyon water. For most of the year, you can only take a shuttle to get to popular trailheads. Arrive very early to minimize wait times (the visitor center parking lot fills up), or come from November to March and drive yourself down the canyon.

FREE PLACE TO CAMP CLOSE TO THE PARK: BLM Circle in La Verkin
GPS: N37.206545' / W113.240797'
~30 minutes to Zion National Park Visitor Center
Plenty of crisscrossed dirt roads so you can find a spot out on your own, or even one overlooking the Virgin River.

Low-Cost Camping Inside the Park
Watchman Campground, $20–$30 per night
Electric and nonelectric sites available. Limited hookups. Dump station available.
GPS: N37.198069' / W112.986715'

Suggested Hikes
THE NARROWS VIA RIVERSIDE WALK: Towering walls and river wading
9.4 miles, moderate, 334 feet elevation gain
This hike is an incredible way to experience Zion National Park. You start at shuttle stop #9, Temple of Sinawava, and head directly into the Virgin River. You can wade and hike as far as Big Springs without a permit. Wear water shoes or shoes you don't mind getting wet and bring trekking poles (no need to rent anything). Always check the weather and the potential for flash floods before entering the canyon.

Believe the hype. It's a humbling experience to swim through a desert river under the golden autumn foliage of cottonwood trees while two thousand feet of Navajo sandstone command a Martian backdrop worthy of a Ray Bradbury novel. We rolled into camp planning to stay three days and ended up hiking and canyoneering for over a week with the help of our friend. Honestly, a burrito and a margarita at Rosita's alone makes it worth the trip. —**CHRIS STEPHAN**

ANGELS LANDING: Adrenaline and heavenly views
5.4 miles, strenuous, 1,488 feet elevation gain
Steep drop-offs and cables to keep balance are trademarks of this incredible trail. If you have a fear of heights or are unsure on your feet, *skip it*. Get off at bus stop #6, zigzag up a mostly paved path, make your way through the Refrigerator Canyon, up more switchbacks, across the spine, and you've reached an iconic view of Zion National Park. Try to catch the first few or last few buses to keep the crowds at bay.

Other Recreational Opportunities

Just outside of Zion National Park, you can find incredible mountain-biking opportunities. In fact, you can camp for free and ride right from your van to the trails. For some really fun moderate flow trails, look no further than the Hurricane Ridge Trail System. If you want something a little more technical, the trails on Gooseberry Mesa draw riders from around the world.

BLACK CANYON OF THE GUNNISON NATIONAL PARK, COLORADO

NATIVE LANDS: Núu-agha-tuvu-pu (Ute)
Sculpted by time and Mother Nature, the Black Canyon of the Gunnison is truly a sight to behold. Over the course of two million years, the mighty Gunnison River carved a space for itself deep in the Precambrian metamorphic rock. Come here to beat the crowds of the more popular parks and watch the stars—the Black Canyon is a certified "Dark Sky" area, making for some of the best stargazing in the country.

FREE PLACE TO CAMP CLOSE TO THE PARK: BLM land near Black Canyon of the Gunnison
Montrose, Colorado
GPS: N38.53065' / W107.720228'
~8 minutes to the South Rim Visitor Center
You can't get more convenient than this camping spot right outside the entrance to the park.
LOW-COST CAMPING INSIDE THE PARK: South Rim Campground $16–$22 per night
Electric hookups
GPS: N38.543148' / W107.688643'

Suggested Hike

GUNNISON ROUTE TRAIL: Into the belly of the beast
1.8 miles, strenuous, 1,781 feet elevation gain
Don't let the short mileage fool you, this is an intense hike down into the canyon. Expect slip-sliding on scree and steep climbing on the way out. Grab a permit early from the visitor center; they are limited. If you decide to drop into the canyon, be on the lookout for poison ivy, and bring extra water.

Other Recreational Opportunities

There are plenty of overlooks to stop at as you drive down the main road that leads all the way to High Point. We suggest exploring around sunrise or sunset for the best views. Don't forget the pooch—dogs on leash are allowed at the overlooks!

The Gunnison River, which winds through the Black Canyon of the Gunnison, is considered a gold-medal wild trout fishery, so bring your fly-fishing gear. While dropping into the canyon is easier said than done, you'll be rewarded with the opportunity to fish for monster rainbow and brown trout.

NORTHWEST

GLACIER NATIONAL PARK, MONTANA

NATIVE LANDS: Niitsítpiis-stahkoii ᖍᒡᐧᒧᐧ ᓴᐦᐧ (Blackfoot/Niitsítapi ᖍᒡᐧᒡᐧ), Ktunaxa
Located in northern Montana near the US-Canadian border is Glacier National Park. The park shares a border with Canada's Waterton Lakes National Park. The setting in this part of the country is something out of a fairy tale. You can hike over seven hundred miles of trails, weaving between peaks that were carved by glaciers, all the while filling up on wild huckleberries. Even if you don't have time to get out of your van, Going-to-the-Sun Road is a sight to behold all in itself.

Please note: Glacier National Park is home to a healthy grizzly bear population, and food storage is required for camping in or near the park. It is best to carry bear spray when recreating in this area.

FREE PLACE TO CAMP CLOSE TO THE PARK: One of the best parts about Glacier National Park is that there is ample free camping on the west side of the park between Columbia Falls and West Glacier. You can camp right on the North Fork of the Flathead River—literally on the border of Glacier National Park. Starting on the west side of the Blankenship Bridge, you can follow the road down and find numerous free camping opportunities. The road is gravel but passable for passenger vehicles.
GPS: West side of Blankenship Bridge, N48.464456' / W114.071732'
You can also camp near the Hungry Horse Reservoir. Once you cross the dam and enter the national forest, you can camp in one of a seemingly endless number of pull-offs on the side of the road. Some are more private than others, but you can find some good

spots with views of the reservoir set against the high peaks of the national park.
GPS: N48.327176' / W113.991668'
LOW-COST CAMPING INSIDE THE PARK: Cut Bank Campground
$10 per night
14 sites, primitive, no hookups, first-come, first-served
GPS: N48.601832' / W113.383769'

Suggested Hikes

GUNSIGHT LAKE VIA THE GUNSIGHT PASS TRAIL: Dense vegetation, pristine rivers, glacier views, and an epic finish
12.9 miles, moderate, 1,742 feet elevation gain
Starting at Going to the Sun Road, you drop down into dense vegetation along the Saint Mary River. As you hike along, it feels like there could be wildlife around every bend. After a few miles the vegetation breaks and the view of Jackson Glacier emerges. From there the views just don't quit.

AVALANCHE LAKE VIA THE TRAIL OF THE CEDARS: Old-growth cedars, hemlock, and a stunning alpine lake

5.7 miles, moderate, 748 feet elevation gain

Starting at the Avalanche parking area, cross the street and enter the Trail of the Cedars. You'll enter an old-growth forest and hike next to a crystal-clear stream fed by melting snow up to an alpine lake. This area is frequently closed for grizzly bear activity and we recommend hiking in a group and with bear spray.

Other Recreational Opportunities

Float and fish the North Fork of the Flathead River right on the border of Glacier National Park. No boat? No problem. You can rent an inflatable kayak for around $60 in West Glacier and hit the water. You'll need to set up a shuttle, but the drive is so pretty you'll forget you've driven the same road twice. Drop a car at the Big Creek River access point (GPS: N48.5990643' / W114.1634239') and then take a second car up to the Polebridge River access point (N48.7824792' / W114.2826166'), inflate your rented kayaks with the provided pump, and hit the water. This is an eighteen-mile float and takes about five hours. There are plenty of options to make it longer or shorter—don't forget your fishing gear!

OLYMPIC NATIONAL PARK, WASHINGTON

NATIVE LANDS: Coast Salish, Klallam, Hoh, Quileute, Chehalis

Diversity is the name of the game in Olympic National Park. The glaciers high atop the Olympic Mountains cascade down into lush temperate rain forest. Those forests eventually end against seventy miles of undeveloped and protected Pacific Northwest coastline. You can reach the Olympic Peninsula a few ways, but we recommend taking the ferry across the Puget Sound from Edmonds to Kingston. This is a spectacular ferry ride that's worth every penny. The fares for the ferry vary by season, the number of people, and vehicle length, but what you'll get in return is a traffic-free ride that provides the opportunity to see dolphins, sea turtles, and even orcas.

FREE PLACE TO CAMP CLOSE TO THE PARK: Hoh River Trust

~7 minutes to the Hoh Rain Forest Visitor Center

Convenient and beautiful, though not suitable for larger RVs

GPS: N47.803744' / W124.096882'

LOW-COST CAMPING INSIDE THE PARK: South Beach Campground $8 per night

Flush toilets, no RV hookups

Camping on a bluff overlooking the Pacific Ocean with beach access.

GPS: N47.565889' / W124.359746'

Suggested Hikes

RIALTO BEACH TRAIL

13.4 miles, moderate, 2,611 feet elevation gain

Rialto Beach Trail is a serene hike along an undeveloped portion of classic Pacific Northwest beach. The hiking can be easy at times but gets more difficult once you reach Hole in the Wall. After this point trekking poles can really come in handy. Due to the topography, it's advisable to carry a tide table and keep an eye on the water. Certain parts of this trail are impassable at high tide. Depending on the time of year, bioluminescent plankton can be found in the water and on the beach. Stick around for sunset to see it illuminate in the waves.

HURRICANE HILL VIA HURRICANE RIDGE TRAIL

3.1 miles, moderate, 797 feet elevation gain

This is the easiest way to get a commanding view of the Olympic Mountains, Puget Sound, and even Vancouver Island. The trail is paved and gets quite busy at times, but it's worth a stop just for the views.

Other Recreational Opportunities

If you have the gear and skills, Olympic National Park's mountains are known for having some of the hardest climbing in the county. The peaks are known for their poor-quality rock and solitary climbing. The highest point in the range is Mount Olympus at a modest 7,969 feet. However, Mount Olympus is heavily glaciated and has the third-largest glacial system in the continental United States.

chapter 12 SUGGESTED ROAD TRIPS AND ITINERARIES

IF YOU'RE A TRAVEL-ADDICT VAN LIFER, then your life can be a satisfying series of scenic and magical road trips—but not without research and planning first. Will you follow the birds and fly south for the winter? Are you a fearless ski bum who loves the cold? Are you trying to visit all the national parks? Making decisions on where to go, and when, can be one of the more stressful parts of living in a van. Do you stay, or do you go?

We've grown accustomed to taking the scenic route. We are able to backpack, fish, mountain bike, climb, and travel intentionally when the scenery isn't speeding by at eighty miles per hour. The road trips we've mapped out below aren't the quickest way to get from one point to the other. They take you on a more interesting journey, stopping at some of

PROTIP

We devour podcasts and audiobooks on long drives. You can sign up with your public library to browse and download their audiobook selection for free. The only catch is the most popular titles usually have a waiting list. A few weeks before a big drive, get on the waiting list for the books you've been looking forward to. By the time you get on the road, they will pop up in your library. Always download books and podcasts offline for travel, so you can binge the whole series without losing service and resorting to local radio (which can also be fun, and it's a great way to get a feel for the area you're driving through).

America's best and sometimes overlooked gems. Plan to complete the whole trip, pick a section, or just find a favorite sport or area from the list. There is a nearly unlimited amount of other activities, hikes, and adventures to access from these itineraries, so fill in the blanks when the opportunity presents itself!

DENVER, COLORADO, TO WHITEFISH, MONTANA

This is a route we hold near and dear to our hearts. We often switch it up, hit different trailheads along the way, take this high alpine pass instead of that one—but the beauty, adventure, and grand views are always present.

STOPS

- Colorado's Rocky Mountain Corridor
- Glenwood Canyon and Glenwood Springs, Colorado
- Fruita, Colorado
- Pinedale and the Wind River Range, Wyoming
- Yellowstone National Park and Gardner, Montana
- Whitefish, Hungry Horse, and Glacier National Park, Montana

FEATURES

- High-altitude hiking
- Mountain biking
- Road cycling
- Rock climbing
- Sightseeing
- Wildlife viewing
- Snow sports
- Whitewater sports
- Flatwater sports

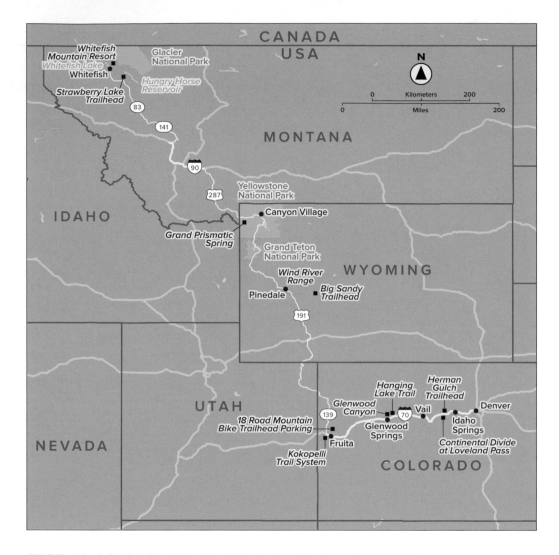

STOP #1: COLORADO'S ROCKY MOUNTAIN CORRIDOR

As you leave the hustle and bustle of Colorado's state capital, the vast plains will start to fade in your rearview mirror. Directly in front of you the Rocky Mountains shoot skyward. At first glance, they don't look all that intimidating, but as your drive trends upward, you won't top out until you reach somewhere between eleven thousand and twelve thousand feet above sea level, depending on your chosen route.

Camping Information

Camping in the Rockies is easy, but camping along the I-70 corridor can be challenging due to private property and development. As you travel farther west in Colorado, boondocking on public land right off the highway becomes more plentiful. You can find some dispersed camping spots on the side of the forest road that leads to the Grey and Torreys Trailhead on the east side of the continental divide (GPS: N39.691230' / W105.804540').

Suggested Hikes

HERMAN GULCH TRAIL: Hike to a classic Rocky Mountain alpine lake.

7 miles, moderate, 1,781 feet elevation gain

SNIKTAU MOUNTAIN TRAIL: Hike up toward Sniktau Mountain (elevation 13,219 feet) high atop the Continental Divide.

7.2 miles, strenuous, 1,587 feet elevation gain

WEST RIDGE TRAIL FROM LOVELAND PASS: An easier alternative to Sniktau Mountain

2.8 miles, moderate, 639 feet elevation gain

Other Recreational Opportunities

- Fish in Clear Creek or Blue River
- Whitewater raft or kayak Clear Creek
- Rock climb in Clear Creek Canyon

- Mountain bike the Keystone Gulch to Soda Creek loop near Keystone Ski Resort for big mountain views
- Partake in the endless front- and backcountry winter sports opportunities

STOP #2: GLENWOOD CANYON AND GLENWOOD SPRINGS, COLORADO

Not the typical landscape you would expect when you think of Colorado, this 12.5-mile canyon was formed by the Colorado River and is a nice stopping point before heading farther down the western slope toward Fruita. Glenwood Springs is home to several developed hot springs and makes a perfect place for a soak and a shower after a long day outdoors.

Suggested Hike

HANGING LAKE TRAIL: A short and steep hike to a true Colorado oasis. Advanced permit required. Note that this area was affected by the Grizzly Creek fire in August 2020.
3 miles, moderate/strenuous, 1,136 feet elevation gain

Camping Information

There is plenty of public land to the west of this area that makes for great camping. The area north of Silt and Rifle have plentiful free camping opportunities (GPS: N39.683130' / W107.650120').

Other Recreational Opportunities

- Soak in the Glenwood Hot Springs pool in Glenwood Springs
- Fish the Colorado River
- Raft or float the Colorado River
- Cross country ski the Grand Mesa Trail system on the way to Fruita

STOP #3: FRUITA, COLORADO

If you're going to pull out your mountain bike for one stop along this road trip, do it in Fruita. Mountain-biking culture is so ingrained in the community here that even the town logo pays homage to the bicycle. After a long day riding, stop in town and grab a cold beverage and a slice at Hot Tomato Pizza, a local favorite.

Camping Information

Camping is available in the North Fruita Desert on BLM land within biking distance of the 18 Road Trail System. As the name suggests, this is a desert and shade can be hard to find (GPS: N39.310153' / W108.703613').

Suggested Rides
PUMPS, BUMPS, AND ROLLERS (PBR) TRAIL VIA PRIME CUT IN THE 18 ROAD TRAIL SYSTEM: It's been said that on this trail you can leave your brakes in the parking lot because you won't need them. You can expect flow, flow, and more flow.
2-mile descent, intermediate (Blue), 425 feet elevation loss
HORSETHIEF BENCH VIA MARY'S LOOP IN THE KOKOPELLI TRAIL SYSTEM: This loop is all about the views. Aside from a short double-black section where most riders hike-a-bike, this is a great trail for intermediate-level riders, with a view overlooking the Colorado River.
3.9 miles, intermediate (Blue/Black), 383 feet elevation gain, 450 feet elevation loss
The Kokopelli system is great for longer rides and has trails for all skill levels.

Other Recreational Opportunities
- Explore Dinosaur National Monument just south of Fruita
- Float the Colorado River from Fruita, Colorado, to Westwater, Utah

STOP #4: PINEDALE, WYOMING, WIND RIVER RANGE
When people think of Wyoming, they usually think of Yellowstone and Grand Teton National Parks. The Wind River Range in central Wyoming is often overlooked—but if you're searching for fewer crowds and the feeling that you've entered the Land Before Time, this is your oasis. Access can be difficult for day hikers, so we recommend back-packing to truly experience this mountain range. The Wind River Range is packed full of high alpine lakes that are an angler's dream. This is grizzly bear country and proper food storage is required.

Camping Information
You can camp at either trailhead before heading out on your journey: Big Sandy Trailhead (GPS: N42.6879785' / W109.2707293') and Elkhart Park Trailhead (GPS: N43.0037451' / W109.7527833'). Camping is also available near Fremont Lake just outside of Pinedale. Fremont lake is Wyoming's second-largest natural lake and is nearly twelve miles long. Wyoming is home to plenty of public lands, and finding free and beautiful boondocking spots is usually easy.

Suggested Backpacking Routes
TITCOMB BASIN VIA ISLAND LAKE: Starting at the Elkhart Park Trailhead (two to four nights)
29.1 miles, strenuous, 3,121 feet elevation gain
THE CIRQUE OF TOWERS VIA BIG SANDY LAKE starting at the Big Sandy Trailhead (two to four nights)
29.8 miles, strenuous, 4,146 feet elevation gain

Other Recreational Opportunities

- Hike to photographer's point
- Swim in Fremont Lake
- Climb the Wolfs Head—a classic alpine trad climb

STOP #5: YELLOWSTONE NATIONAL PARK

Yellowstone can be crowded depending on the time of year that you visit, but it's one of our country's most unique parks and should be on everyone's bucket list. Check out chapter 11 for detailed information about what to do in Yellowstone.

STOP #6: WHITEFISH/HUNGRY HORSE/GLACIER NATIONAL PARK, MONTANA

This area offers activities for every type of outdoor enthusiast. This entire area is grizzly country! Food storage is required and it's recommended that you carry bear spray anytime you're recreating away from town. We cover what to do in Glacier National Park in chapter 11. In this chapter we'll cover what you can do outside the national park.

Camping Information

There is plenty of public land around Whitefish, Hungry Horse, and Glacier National Park. We've added few a camping locations under Glacier National Park in chapter 11. It's a bit of a drive out of town, but there is ample boondocking near Hungry Horse Reservoir (GPS: N48.3380588' / W114.0127032').

Suggested Hike

STRAWBERRY LAKE: A strenuous hike to a cool mountain lake that's perfect for summer swimming
6 miles, strenuous, 1,912 feet elevation gain

Other Recreational Opportunities

- Float the Whitefish River
- Mountain bike or hitch a ride on the lift to the top of Whitefish Mountain Resort

MOAB, UTAH, TO YOSEMITE NATIONAL PARK, CALIFORNIA

Sure, there's a quicker way to get from eastern Utah to Yosemite National Park, but where's the fun in that? This road trip will take you through Utah's Mighty 5 national parks in addition to Grand Staircase-Escalante National Monument. From there you'll continue the journey southwest until you find yourself sitting in the heart of the Yosemite Valley in California's impressive Sierra Nevada.

STOPS

- Moab, Utah
- Little Wildhorse Canyon, Utah
- Capitol Reef National Park, Utah
- Grand Staircase-Escalante, Utah
- Bryce Canyon National Park, Utah
- Zion National Park, Utah
- Horseshoe Bend, Arizona
- Grand Canyon National Park, Arizona
- Las Vegas, Nevada
- Death Valley National Park, California
- Yosemite National Park, California

FEATURES

- Slot canyons
- Canyoneering
- Hiking
- Mountain biking
- Climbing
- Sightseeing

PROTIP

We're able to get to know these areas so much better because we live there for extended periods of time, versus a few days on vacation. We've spent weeks on BLM land, watching the seasons change. Our favorite spots vary based on the season. In the summer the Pacific Northwest can't be beat. In the winter you'll find us in the desert of west Texas or southern Utah or Arizona. The eastern Sierras in California also hold a very special place in our hearts. **—THE FOXES**

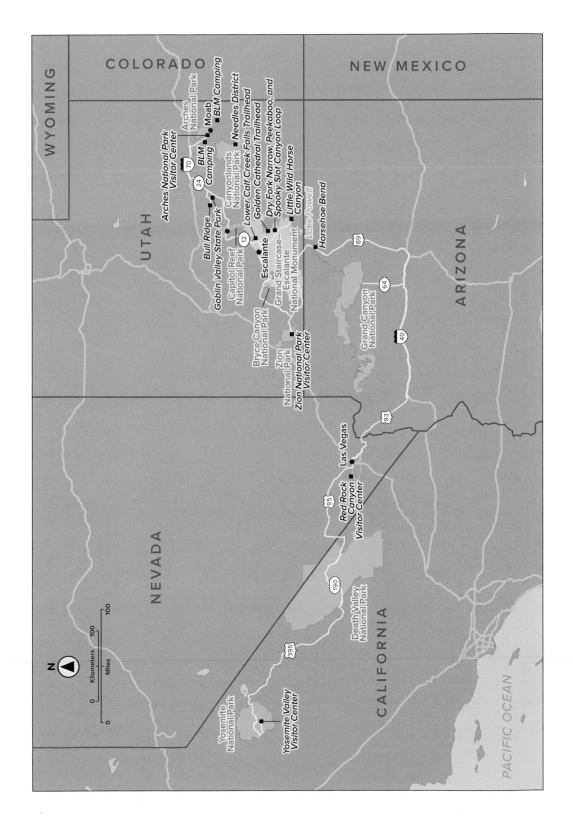

STOP #1: CANYONLANDS AND ARCHES NATIONAL PARKS, AND MOAB, UTAH

Moab is a wonderful little desert town in eastern Utah that sits at the doorstep of both Arches and Canyonlands National Parks. Moab is a great place to stock up on any last-minute things before heading out. If you follow our route exactly, Moab is also the largest town you will see for quite a while. For information regarding Canyonlands National Park, refer to the chapter 11.

Camping Information

This area of Utah has abundant public land that allows free and legal camping. This area is so extensive that we recommend downloading the Motor Vehicle Use Map of the area for information on where to camp. There are large swaths of BLM land to the north of Moab between Moab and Interstate 70. This is one of the many locations where you can camp (GPS: N38.696832' / W109.6981'). This location is popular with people visiting the area. If you find yourself in Moab in the summertime, we recommend heading for higher ground and to cooler temperatures. You can take the La Sal Mountain loop road just south of town straight up into the La Sal Mountains. From here, you can find shade, cooler temperatures, and an impressive view of the Utah desert below. You can camp off the road

once you enter the national forest. Here are the approximate GPS coordinates for camping in the La Sal Mountains: N38.476741' / W109.343744'.

Suggested Hike

DELICATE ARCH: A short hike to a unique natural arch with a view of the La Sal Mountains
3 miles, easy/moderate, 610 feet elevation gain

Other Recreational Opportunities

- Rent a UTV in Moab and go off-roading in Sand Flats Recreation Area
- Raft, swim, or float the Colorado River, which runs through town
- Mountain bike on signature Utah slick rock in one of Moab's extensive trail systems
- Rock climb in Bears Ears National Monument a few hours south of town

STOP #2: LITTLE WILDHORSE CANYON AND BELL CANYON, UTAH

Little Wildhorse Canyon is a one-stop destination for exploring the canyon. This canyon is an incredible intro to Utah's endless amount of slot canyons. Until recently, this hike was accessible to just about everyone. However, now there's a rock jam near the beginning of

the canyon that was caused by a flash flood in the spring of 2020. Most hikers will be able to find a way around or over the obstruction, but this could be a deal-breaker for those without sure footing.

Avoid slot canyons if there is any chance of rain in the area—at all. Any chance? Don't go. Slot canyons will flood very quickly and become extremely dangerous and even deadly.

Camping Information

This region in Utah consists of large areas of public land. Once you leave Interstate 70, you will see plenty of opportunities for boondocking in the desert. If you want something a little less primitive, Goblin Valley State Park is just twelve miles down the road and has a campground with full hookups for around $30 per night. There are large free-camping areas established between the state park and Little Wild Horse Canyon as well (GPS: N38.5804617' / W110.7730406').

Suggested Hike

LITTLE WILDHORSE CANYON TO BELL CANYON LOOP

8 miles, moderate, 787 feet elevation gain

If you want to do something a little shorter, you can hike just Little Wildhorse Canyon as an out-and-back. This way the hike can be as long or as short as you'd like. We suggest hiking this loop counterclockwise.

Other Recreational Opportunities

- 4x4 off-roading in the Utah Desert
- Visit Goblin Valley State Park

STOP #3: CAPITOL REEF NATIONAL PARK, UTAH

As you cruise along Utah State Highway 24 from Little Wildhorse Canyon to Grand Stair-case Escalante, you'll drive right through Capitol Reef National Park. Capitol Reef, according to the National Park Service, is "a hidden treasure filled with cliffs, canyons, domes, and bridges in the Waterpocket Fold, a geologic monocline (a wrinkle on the earth) extending almost 100 miles." Why not stop and explore?

Camping Information

Like most national parks, there are several developed campgrounds inside the park. The closest to Highway 24 is the Fruita Campground, where the nightly fee is $20. There are no hookups in the Fruita Campground. We recommend camping for free in Dixie National Forest (GPS: N38.165430' / W111.324560'). You'll see plenty of boondocking spots right off of Highway 12 between Capitol Reef and Boulder, Utah. Here, you'll have much cooler temperatures and a sweeping view of the desert below.

Suggested Hikes

HICKMAN BRIDGE TRAIL: A short and scenic hike to a beautiful natural bridge
1.8 miles, easy, 442 feet elevation gain

CASSIDY ARCH VIA FRYING PAN TRAIL: A more immersive hike through a unique environment and geologic features leading to Cassidy Arch
8.3 miles, strenuous, 2,391 feet elevation qain

Other Recreational Opportunities

- Watch the stars at this International Dark Sky Park
- Explore the park by horseback
- Canyoneering—enjoy the park by rappelling in from above
- Grab your crash pad and go bouldering outside Bicknell

STOP #4: GRAND STAIRCASE-ESCALANTE NATIONAL MONUMENT, UTAH

Encompassing nearly one million acres of public land, Grand Staircase-Escalante National Monument is a diverse wonderland dotted with arches, natural bridges, slot canyons, and fascinating rock formations. Spending a night under the stars here makes it easy to see why tribes such as the Ute, Pueblos, and Southern Paiute found this place so spiritual. You could spend years exploring this area—if you want to narrow your visit down to one general area, head to Hole-in-the-Rock Road. This 62-mile road stretches from Escalante, Utah, all the way to Hole-in-the-Rock on the western shore of Lake Powell. Please note that sudden rain can make this road completely impassable. Check the forecast before losing cell service.

Camping Information

There are endless primitive camping opportunities off of Hole-in-the-Rock-Road. You can find excellent camping starting at the beginning of the road (GPS: N37.7267725' / W111.5308327').

Suggested Hikes

DRY FORK NARROWS, PEEKABOO, AND SPOOKY SLOT CANYON LOOP: This lollipop hike to three separate slot canyons is the perfect intro to Grand Staircase-Escalante National Monument.
6.3 miles, strenuous (depending on route), 738 feet elevation gain
Dry Fork Narrows is easy and can be accessed by most hikers. Peekaboo Slot Canyon has one obstacle at the beginning or very end depending on which way you access it. The obstacle is an almost vertical Class 3 scramble that lasts for about ten feet. This can be challenging for dogs and kids. Spooky Slot Canyon is the most difficult of the three. Spooky is also very narrow, and you'll have to be comfortable in tight spaces for long

periods of time to complete this canyon. There are several Class 3 sections inside the canyon that make for a really fun canyon scramble. We don't recommend bringing a dog into Spooky. You'll need to lift them over your head in several sections.

LOWER CALF CREEK FALLS: A short hike to a rare desert waterfall right off the main road. 6.7 miles, moderate, 521 feet elevation gain

Recommended Backpacking Route
THE GOLDEN CATHEDRAL TRAIL
9.1 miles, strenuous, 1,581 feet elevation gain

While you can easily make this a day hike, we recommend spending a night in the Golden Cathedral to really absorb its beauty. You'll start this hike off with a 1,500-foot descent into a beautiful river canyon where you'll find a desert oasis called Neon Canyon. This hike is more strenuous than you'd expect due to sandy sections, lack of shade (at the top), and difficult route finding. The hike ends at the Golden Cathedral, which you need to see to believe. Thrill seekers can even rappel down through a dome directly into the Golden Cathedral.

Other Recreational Opportunities

- Enjoy seemingly endless canyoneering opportunities
- Enjoy spotting wildlife while rock climbing on the scenic soft sandstone
- OHV/4x4 near Hole in the Rock Road

STOP #5: BRYCE CANYON NATIONAL PARK, UTAH

As you depart Grand Staircase-Escalante, you might be thinking that you're ready for different scenery. Bryce Canyon has you covered. Bryce Canyon is home to the largest concentration of hoodoos (irregular rock formations) found anywhere on earth. In fact, it feels a little bit like you're on the moon. If you want a novel type of experience, hire a guide and explore the park on horseback.

Camping Information
Bryce Canyon is home to two campgrounds that are both within close proximity to the visitor center. The North Campground is available on a first-come, first-served basis and is $20 for a tent site and $30 for an RV site per night. The Sunset Campground accepts reservations and the costs are the same. There are free camping opportunities in the adjacent Dixie National Forest (GPS: N37.626331' / W112.228073').

Suggested Hikes
SUNSET TO SUNRISE VIA THE PAVED RIM TRAIL: This is an easy paved hike that offers spectacular views into Bryce Canyon. It is the perfect hike if you just plan on stopping for an hour to see what Bryce Canyon has to offer, and this is also the best place (as the name suggests) to catch a beautiful sunrise or sunset.
1 mile, easy, 34 feet elevation gain

FAIRYLAND LOOP: You'll wind through pink cliffs and the famous Bryce Canyon hoodoos on this stunning loop through the canyon. This is the perfect day hike to get a taste of the park. The hike includes a short walk along the canyon rim before descending into the belly of the canyon. You'll encounter a short spur trail to Tower Bridge. The view is worth the extra distance. Bring your camera and plenty of water.
8 miles, strenuous, 1,716 feet elevation gain

Other Recreational Opportunities
- Snowshoe/cross-country ski on the plateau
- Enjoy the park on horseback
- Mountain bike Thunder Mountain
- OHV/4x4 in the surrounding desert

STOP #6: ZION NATIONAL PARK, UTAH
Check out chapter 11 for what to do in Zion National Park.

STOP #7: HORSESHOE BEND, ARIZONA
Even if you're not familiar with this iconic bend in the mighty Colorado River, you've likely seen a picture. Horseshoe Bend in Page, Arizona, is a great place to stop and stretch your legs while on your way to the Grand Canyon. It is somewhat of a one-trick pony, pun intended, but it offers a unique and scenic overlook that's worth the stop. There is a $10 parking fee that includes access to the overlook.

Camping Information
Just twelve minutes north of Horseshoe Bend (GPS: N36.936089' / W111.503441') you can find free camping within walking distance of swimming opportunities in Lake Powell. The

road gets sandy and can be impassible when wet. It's best to walk sandy sections of the road to check their condition before driving through them.

Suggested Hike

HORSESHOE BEND TRAIL: This is a fully ADA-compliant trail that can be accessed by anyone! The distance noted below is round-trip from the parking area to the Horseshoe Bend lookout. However, for those looking to escape the crowds and explore a little farther, you may walk around the rim for as long as you'd like.
1.4 miles, easy, 380 feet elevation gain

Other Recreational Opportunities

- Helicopter tours—a bird's-eye view
- Go horseback riding around the canyon rim
- Rafting trips—rafting the Colorado River is pure joy

STOP #8: GRAND CANYON NATIONAL PARK, ARIZONA

See chapter 11 for the lowdown on Grand Canyon National Park.

STOP #9: LAS VEGAS, NEVADA

What's an outdoor adventure road trip without a stop in Vegas? Seriously though, even if Las Vegas isn't your scene, it makes a great rest stop between the Grand Canyon and Death Valley National Park. Believe it or not, you can usually find a cheap room right on the strip that makes for a great stopping point to take a shower and catch a show. Las Vegas also has a dirty little secret. There are a ton of outdoor gems just waiting to be explored. Located less than seventeen miles from downtown Las Vegas is Red Rocks National Conservation Area. Here, you'll find top-notch rock climbing on sandstone and scenic hiking. And (we can't resist) what happens in Red Rocks, stays in Red Rocks.

Camping Information

You can camp just twenty miles from the Las Vegas Strip at the Red Rock Canyon Campground located in Red Rocks National Conservation Area (GPS: N36.1313889' / W115.3838889'). The cost is $10 per night and reservations are required. This campground regularly fills up with rock climbers, and you'll want to make reservations as far in advance as possible. You can also find some free camping opportunities to the southwest in Lovell Canyon (GPS: N36.059785' / W115.561924').

Suggested Hike

ICE BOX CANYON TRAIL: A great intro hike in Red Rocks National Conservation Area with some fun scrambling. Just like the name suggests, you'll hike into a cool and shady box

canyon that will make you feel like you're worlds away from the hustle and bustle of the Las Vegas Strip. While the canyon rarely sees sunlight and is much cooler than the open desert, you do have to cross the hot desert to access it. Bring plenty of water.
2.3 miles, moderate, 577 feet elevation gain

Other Recreational Opportunities

- Rock climb with layers of earth stacked around you
- Bike the entire paved portion of the South Rim (and use the bus to get back)
- Take a guided horseback ride along the North Rim

PROTIP

Our favorite mode of outdoor adventure is multiday paddling on rivers in our inflatable tandem kayaks because of the pace, the effort vs. reward, and ability to pack everything we need for four people and a dog for up to a week and not have to carry it! This country is full of amazing wilderness—every state has it and we love respectfully recreating in all of it. **—COLIN BOYD & SOFI ALDINIO**

STOP #10: DEATH VALLEY NATIONAL PARK, CALIFORNIA

Death Valley is the lowest, hottest, and driest national park. Depending on what time of the year you make this road trip, you may not even want to get out of your car. In the summer, temperatures regularly reach 120 degrees Fahrenheit—make sure your engine is in working order before taking the drive. Detouring through the park also takes you on a more scenic route to Yosemite National Park.

Camping Information

This is one of the few national parks that offers free camping! During the summer months temperatures can hit 120 degrees Fahrenheit, dropping only to 100 at night. Due to these unfavorable conditions, there are only a four campgrounds open in the summer months. All campgrounds are available on a first-come, first-served basis except the Furnace Creek Campground, which accepts reservations from October 15 to April 15. Emigrant, Wildrose, Thorndike, and Mahogany Campgrounds are all free. Furnace Creek, Sunset, Texas Springs, Stovepipe Wells, and Mesquite Creek all offer sites for $16 per night or less.

Suggested Hike

BADWATER BASIN SALT FLATS TRAIL: The hike to the Badwater Basin Salt Flats offers a truly unique experience found only in Death Valley. In fact, this hike will take you to the lowest point in North America, at 282 feet below sea level. Because of the climate here, this hike is best done during the cooler months. The expansive salt flats appear to go on forever.
1.8 miles, moderate, 9 feet elevation gain

Other Recreational Opportunities

- Take a *Star Wars* tour of Death Valley
- Bike along any of the winding desert roads

STOP #11: YOSEMITE NATIONAL PARK, CALIFORNIA]

You did it! You made it to Yosemite National Park in California. If you need some helpful hints on Yosemite, head on over to chapter 11.

SEATTLE, WASHINGTON, TO SAN FRANCISCO, CALIFORNIA

The legendary Pacific Northwest. The mystical trees, sprawling beaches, and bountiful outstanding camping make it a wonderful place to get lost (or just follow the itinerary). Jump on Highway 101, spend some time among the giants, then revitalize your soul in the sea.

STOPS
- Seattle, Washington
- Port Angeles, Washington
- La Push, Washington; and Olympic National Park
- Thor's Well, Oregon
- Yachats, Oregon
- Redwood State and National Parks, California
- San Francisco, California

FEATURES
- Hiking
- Backpacking
- Beach camping
- Alpine climbing
- Surfing
- Scenic driving
- Sightseeing
- Swimming
- Wildlife viewing

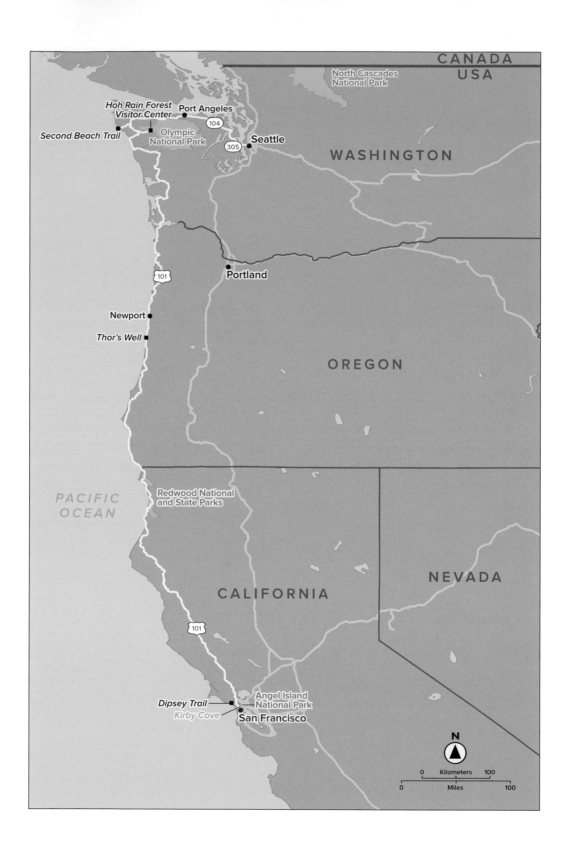

STOP #1: SEATTLE, WASHINGTON

Seattle can be hectic and plagued with awful traffic. If you're in the area, we recommend hopping into the city, grabbing some delicious food and a few pounds of locally roasted coffee, and hitting the road ASAP. While it is possible to boondock in Seattle, we don't recommend it. Consider getting an Airbnb in a neighborhood like Capitol Hill and using that as your basecamp for exploration. While you're living the city life, book ferry tickets from Edmonds to Kingston. This is the best way to get from the city to the Olympic Peninsula. Price varies by length of vehicle, and number of people. The ferry runs several times daily.

Camping Information

Camping near any major metropolitan area can be challenging and Seattle is no exception. Your best bet here is to find camp after you take the Ferry from Edmonds to Kingston. Or treat yourself to a roof and four walls for the night. If you plan on finding camp after you take the ferry, you can camp at Kitsap Memorial State Park (GPS: N47.8179069' / W122.6511436'). Rates vary from $12 to $50 per night depending on desired site and time of year. Reservations are required.

Suggested Hike

DISCOVER PARK AND LIGHTHOUSE LOOP TRAIL: This urban park offers big views of the Puget Sound and Bainbridge Island. Walk to the beach and view the West Point Lighthouse. You'll also have the opportunity to view wildlife along this beachy Pacific Northwest trail.
4.4 miles, easy, 472 feet elevation gain

Other Recreational Opportunities

- Road bike from Seattle to Discovery Park along the seaboard
- Catch some whale tales in the Puget Sound
- Kayak around the mystical San Juan Islands

STOP #2: PORT ANGELES, WASHINGTON

Once you get off the ferry in Kingston and make your way toward Highway 101, the highway that you'll take all the way to San Francisco, you can make a stop in Port Angeles. This little town on the coast is a great place to grab any last-minute groceries and gas before heading farther west toward the Pacific coast. From here you can also grab the international ferry over to Victoria, British Columbia, on Vancouver island. Port Angeles is also a basecamp for accessing Olympic National Park.

Camping Information

If you need a place to park for the night, there's a rest stop on Highway 101 (GPS: N48.106770' / W123.348410') that allows overnight parking and makes for an easy stopping point close to the main road. There is RV parking as well.

Suggested Hike

DEVIL'S PUNCHBOWL VIA SPRUCE RAILROAD TRAIL: This dog-friendly paved trail meanders around the stunning shores of Lake Crescent. It can be walked or biked and made much longer if desired. The Spruce Railroad Trail is part of the much-larger Olympic Discovery Trail. Don't forget your bathing suit—Devil's Punchbowl is the perfect place for a dip in the summertime.
2.4 miles, easy, 144 feet elevation gain

Other Recreational Opportunities

- Fish for Dungeness crab, or try some at their annual October festival
- A sunrise kayak trip could be the perfect wildlife-viewing opportunity

- Explore the winding mountain-bike trails at Dry Hill
- Snowshoe Hurricane Ridge in Olympic National Park

STOP #3: OLYMPIC NATIONAL PARK, WASHINGTON

Olympic National Park is amazingly diverse. You'll encounter mountains, rain forest, and moody Pacific Northwest beaches. We cover Olympic National Park in chapter 11.

STOP #4: LA PUSH, WASHINGTON

La Push is a small, often foggy village surrounded by Olympic National Park. Stop here to access quintessential Pacific Northwest beaches and maybe encounter some werewolves.

Camping Information

Since La Push is located in the Quileute Reservation surrounded by Olympic National Park, you won't be able to camp for free without traveling farther south. However, if you don't mind a short walk, you can tent camp on Second Beach. Grab a permit from the ranger station ahead of time. You can also camp at the nearby Mora Campground (GPS: N47.9181983' / W124.6091893') for $20 per night. Reservations are required in peak season, which is generally mid-March through mid-September.

Suggested Hike

Second Beach Trail is a great way to explore the beach in Olympic National Park. You can complete this hike as an easy out-and-back. Depending on the time of year, you may be able to see bioluminescent plankton in the water or on the beach.
1.9 miles, easy, 282 feet elevation gain

Other Recreational Opportunities

• Hire a charter boat and go deep-sea fishing
• Go for a dip at any one of the beaches

From La Push this route turns into a "choose your own" type of adventure. From here you can continue down Highway 101 soaking up everything the coast has to offer. Or you can cut east, drive through Portland, stop and get Fried Egg I'm in Love (a favorite cafe) for breakfast, and be on your way. Either route makes for a great road trip option. All roads lead back to Newport, Oregon, and the quiet central Oregon coast.

STOP #5: YACHATS, OREGON

With so much commercialization along the Pacific coast, Yachats (pronounced YAH-hots), Oregon, is a breath of fresh air. Yachats feels genuine, the food is great, and the view is spectacular. What more would you want in a seaside town? Its nickname is the Gem of the Oregon Coast, and it lives up to it. Grab a cocktail and a bite to eat at the Drift Inn while you're passing through. Depending on when you're there, you can catch some live music in their eclectic dining room.

Camping Information

As you drive down the central Oregon coast, you'll see plenty of boondocking opportunities. It's hard to determine the legality of many of the pull-offs so we can't in good conscience recommend any of them. If you are in doubt of where to camp, there are plenty of legal camping opportunities in Siuslaw National Forest just to the east.

Suggested Hikes

CAPTAIN COOK TRAIL TO THOR'S WELL: A great trail right off the road that features unique rock features and tide pools
0.6 miles, easy, 95 feet elevation gain

HECETA LIGHTHOUSE TRAIL: An easy hike to a classic Oregon Lighthouse
0.9 miles, easy, 131 feet elevation gain

Other Recreational Opportunities

- Wildlife viewing
- Enjoy both ocean and freshwater fishing opportunities
- Mountain bike the Cape Mountain Trail System

STOP #6: REDWOOD NATIONAL AND STATE PARKS, CALIFORNIA

As you meander down the coast and eventually cross into California, the redwoods are not to be missed. You'll be able to weave your way in and out of a patchwork of protected parks and redwood groves. We cover Redwood National and State Parks in chapter 11.

STOP #7: SAN FRANCISCO, CALIFORNIA

Oh, San Francisco! You've made it to the City by the Bay. Take advantage of the surprising amount of outdoor adventure opportunities the Bay Area has to offer. By the way, if you've made it this far, San Francisco is only a four-hour drive away from Yosemite National Park, where you can pick up another one of our road trips, from Yosemite National Park to Moab, Utah.

Camping Information

As with most big cities, boondocking can be hard to find. We recommend reserving a spot at Kirby Cove Campground. $30 per night.

Suggested Hike

THE DIPSEA TRAIL: A hike through some of California's most famous coastal redwoods in Muir Woods National Monument to Stinson Beach
9.7 miles, strenuous, 2,545 feet elevation gain

Other Recreational Opportunities

- Visit Kirby Cover in Golden Gate National Recreation Area for an unequalled view of the Golden Gate Bridge
- Surfing in Pacifica, Rockaway Beach, or Linda Mar
- Take a ferry ride to Angel Island State Park, the largest natural island in the San Francisco Bay
- Visit Purisima Creek Redwoods Preserve for a hike or bike through massive coast redwoods

SHENANDOAH NATIONAL PARK, VIRGINIA, TO CHARLESTON, SOUTH CAROLINA

This trip will have you traversing the rolling and panoramic Blue Ridge Mountains before you cut southwest and make a break for the ocean. Try this one in the fall when the air gets cooler, the humidity subsides, and the leaves start to show off.

STOPS

- Shenandoah National Park, Virginia
- Roanoke, Virginia
- Roan Mountain, Tennessee
- Gatlinburg and Great Smoky Mountains National Park, Tennessee
- Asheville, North Carolina
- Brevard, North Carolina
- Congaree National Park, South Carolina
- Charleston, South Carolina

FEATURES

- Hiking
- Mountain biking
- Backpacking
- Rock climbing
- Surfing
- Fishing

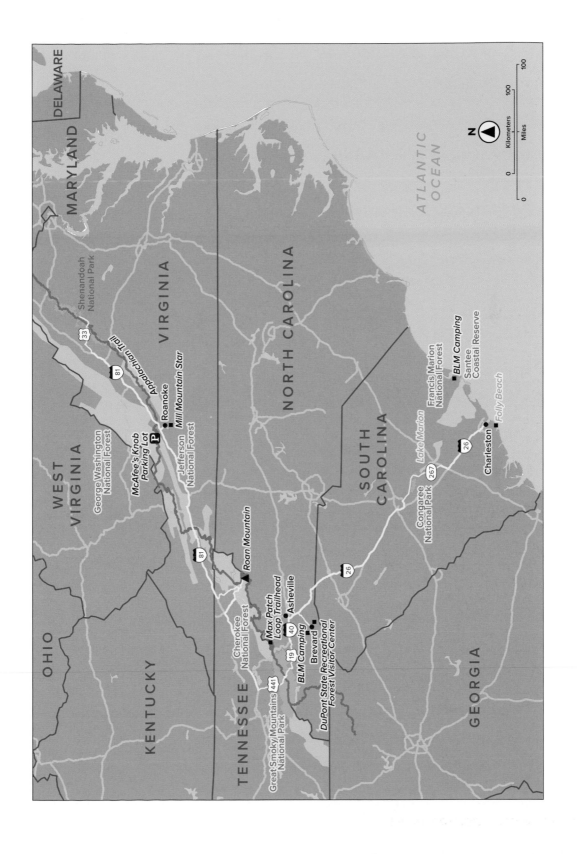

STOP #1: SHENANDOAH NATIONAL PARK, VIRGINIA

The rolling Blue Ridge Mountains are a perfect way to kick off a road trip. Lucky for you, we've covered Shenandoah National Park in chapter 11.

STOP #2: ROANOKE, VIRGINIA

The city of Roanoke lives and breathes the outdoor lifestyle. You can use the city as a basecamp for all of the outdoor adventures surrounding the area. If you need to stop and get a little work done, Sweet Donkey Coffee is the place for Wi-Fi and a good cup of bean water.

Camping Information

While maybe not the most convenient boondocking location in the area, Pines Campground is a great spot (GPS: N37.605' / W80.075829'). The Pines is a free national forest campground in George Washington National Forest that offers pit toilets, fire rings, and peace and quiet.

Suggested Hikes

The Roanoke area is home to many trails but none are more iconic than the Appalachian Trail. The Triple Crown is comprised of three separate hikes that are connected by the Appalachian Trail. These can be hiked separately as day hikes or hiked together as an overnight trip.

DRAGON'S TOOTH TRAIL: This is a great hike that can be done relatively quickly. Scramble up the "Dragon's Tooth" at the top for an excellent sunrise or sunset view.
4.1 miles, moderate–strenuous, 1,227 feet elevation gain

TINKER CLIFFS VIA ANDY LANE TRAIL: From the top of the cliffs, you'll have sweeping views into Catawba Valley and the McAfee Knob area.
7 miles, moderate, 1,902 feet elevation gain

MCAFEE KNOB VIA THE APPALACHIAN TRAIL: The most popular section of the Triple Crown and generally considered the most photographed spot along the entire Appalachian Trail.
8.1 miles, moderate, 1,843 feet elevation gain

VIRGINIA'S TRIPLE CROWN: Hike all three! This loop will minimize backtracking, allowing you to hike along the Appalachian Trail for several miles.
35.1 miles, strenuous, 7,870 feet elevation gain

Other Recreational Opportunities

- Go mountain biking on Mill Mountain or in Douthat State Park
- Catch fish at Carvins Cove Natural Reserve
- Rock climb in the Roanoke River Gorge
- Dial in your paddling skills on one of many classic whitewater runs

STOP #3: GREAT SMOKY MOUNTAINS NATIONAL PARK, TENNESSEE

We love these foggy giants. We cover Great Smoky Mountains National Park in chapter 11.

STOP #4: ASHEVILLE, NORTH CAROLINA

As you travel through the mountains and across Tennessee's border with North Carolina, you'll begin to smell the barbecue. Asheville is a really fun town and the food is absolutely incredible. Stop and grab some grub from 12 Bones Smokehouse. You can thank us later.

Camping Information

You'll need to do a little driving to find prime camping in this area, but once you're out of town, you'll have plenty of options. North Mills River Campground (GPS: N35.407241' / W82.644042') is a nice secluded camping option right on the banks of the North Fork Mills River. Bring your fishing gear if you plan to camp here. Spots can be reserved for $24 to $40 per night. If you want a free option, you can camp near Max Pax at the Harmon Den dispersed camping area (GPS: N35.762689' / W82.983727').

Suggested Hike
MAX PATCH: One of the most popular sections of the Appalachian Trail in North Carolina. You'll hike to huge open, grassy balds with stellar views of the Smoky Mountains.
1.5 miles, easy, 288 feet elevation gain

Other Recreational Opportunities
- Float on the French Broad River
- Fish the French Broad River
- Rock climb in the Linville Gorge

STOP #5: BREVARD, NORTH CAROLINA
Brevard is all about the mountain biking. You can bike to town and grab a beer at the Hub (bike shop with a bar) on your way back from the trails.

Camping Information
There are a lot of boondocking sites in Pisgah National Forest, but they can be tricky to find. Start by checking Avery Creek (GPS: N35.29888' / W82.73839') and the surrounding area. The Davidson River Campground has all types of sites ranging from $24 to $48 per night. They even have hot showers.

Suggested Mountain Bike Rides
DUPONT STATE RECREATIONAL FOREST: Great moderate singletrack with a few technical sections. The trail system here is extensive and it's best to carry a map or GPS.
DUPONT RIDGELINE: A great intro to the area
6.3 miles, moderate (blue), 697 feet elevation gain
BLACK MOUNTAIN LOOP: A taste of Pisgah National Forest riding with an epic downhill
12.2 miles, strenuous, 2,244 feet elevation gain

Other Recreational Opportunities
- Fish the Davidson River

STOP #6: CONGAREE NATIONAL PARK, SOUTH CAROLINA
Congaree is a great park and it's not to be missed! We cover this park in chapter 11.

STOP #7: CHARLESTON, SOUTH CAROLINA
You've made it to the big city! It might be shocking after spending so much time in small towns and off the grid altogether. Charleston is the largest city in South Carolina and it has a lot of personality. Take some time to enjoy the food, music, and sense of community that makes Charleston unique. When you're done with the city life, head south and relax in the small coastal town of Folly Beach.

Camping Information

Charleston is just south of Francis Marion National Forest. We recommend camping for free in the Santee Coastal Reserve Wildlife Management Area (GPS: N33.154879' / W79.368238'). Camping here requires a permit, but the permits are free and available onsite.

Suggested Hike

AWENDAW PASSAGE (PALMETTO TRAIL): The Palmetto Trail runs for 425 miles and traverses the state of South Carolina. Awendaw Passage is the final section of this thru-hike. Located in Francis Marion National Forest, you'll enjoy views of the beautiful South Carolina swamp and a chance to see plenty of wildlife. If you wish, you can also bike this trail. 7 miles, easy, 131 feet elevation gain

Recreational Opportunities

- Explore the West Ashley Greenway
- Paddle the estuaries near Folly Beach
- Surf at Folly Beach
- Sea kayak to Morris Island and the Morris Island Light House

MILLINOCKET, MAINE, TO DEEP CREEK LAKE, MARYLAND

Once you plug into the van life world, you will start to notice a trend. There are plenty of van lifers out west and not nearly the same popularity in the east. With a larger population density, the East Coast should be teeming with van lifers. The answer to this riddle is simple: It's easier to live in a van out west. There's more space, fewer people, and vast public lands. But visiting the East Coast in your van can be just as magical. There is a large concentration of cities to explore, beautiful national parks, delicious seafood, and canopied hiking. Our suggestion? Skip the bugs, and some of the humidity, and plan a trip for fall. The leaves will explode with color, the apple picking will be top-notch, and the cider will be the perfect temperature.

STOPS

- Millinocket, Maine
- Acadia National Park, Maine
- Mount Washington, New Hampshire
- Portland, Maine
- Provincetown, Massachusetts
- Shawangunk Mountains, New York
- Hawk's Nest Highway, Liberty to Port Jervis, New York
- Deep Creek Lake, Maryland

FEATURES

- Hiking
- Mountain biking
- Backpacking
- Rock climbing
- Leaf peeping
- Fishing
- Whitewater and flatwater sports

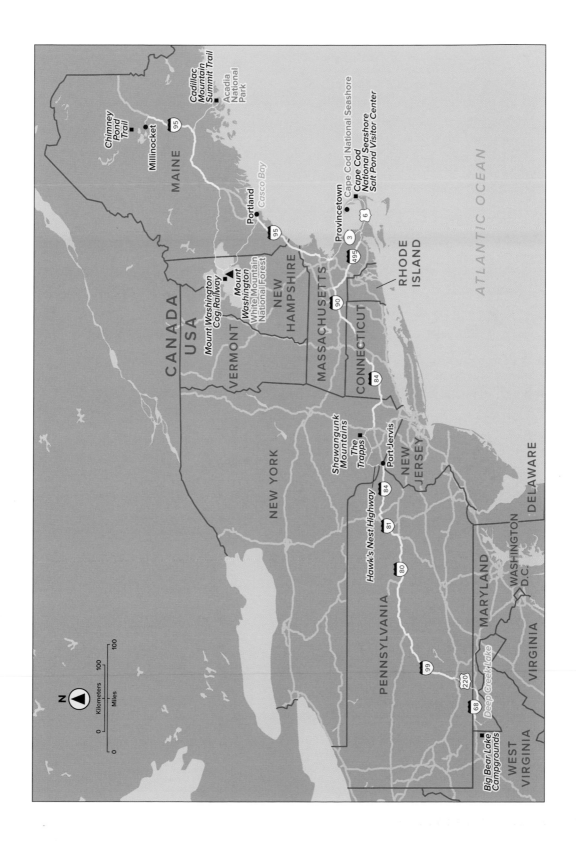

STOP #1: MILLINOCKET, MAINE

With the terminus of the Appalachian Trail just a few miles north, you will catch many a hiker finishing their 2,000+-mile journey relaxing in town before returning to real life (what is real life, anyway?). Take in the atmosphere with a coffee at the AT Cafe, then head out for some big adventure days.

Camping Information

How does a scenic quiet beach in the middle of nowhere sound? Camp at Penobscot River Corridor, Omaha Beach. Sites can be purchased for $12 per night, and the only amenities you'll find are an outhouse and endless beauty (GPS: N45.768078' / W68.940853').

COLIN BOYD & SOFI ALDINIO

Suggested Hike

MOUNT KATAHDIN AND HAMLIN PEAK LOOP: A challenging hike that summits some of the tallest peaks in Maine, including Baxter Peak, the terminus of the Appalachian Trail (on Mount Katahdin). It features a knife-edge that'll make you forget you're not in the Rockies. Alpine start (leave as early in the morning as possible) to complete this one safely.
11.5 miles, strenuous, 4,475 elevation gain

Other Recreational Opportunities

- Snowmobile to dining options (for real)
- Whitewater raft on Penobscot River
- Swim, paddle, or float in one of the many lakes in the area

STOP #2: ACADIA NATIONAL PARK, MAINE

Acadia continues to make the list of Top Ten Most Visited National Parks (according to nps .gov numbers) through the years. It has varied landscapes, interesting wildlife, and adorable surrounding towns. Bring the pups as there's plenty of trails where they're allowed (one hundred miles of hiking trails, forty-five miles of carriage roads) and three campgrounds where pets are welcome.

Camping Information

Finding places to camp for free isn't easy around this part of the coast. Our best suggestion is to book a few nights inside the park, so you can really dive in but don't have to drive an hour or so every day to get back (unless you're willing to call a Walmart parking lot your home for a few nights—no judgment!). Try out one of the four campgrounds in the park, reserve early, and expect to pay between $20 and $30 per night.

Suggested Hike

CADILLAC MOUNTAIN SOUTH RIDGE TRAIL LOOP: View the sunrise from Cadillac Mountain! You can be the first person in the entire United States to view the sunrise from the top of this mountain (mid-October through early March). While you can drive to the top, we recommend waking and walking before the sun is up and catching the sunrise from the summit. Take the South Ridge Trail up, leaving yourself plenty of time to summit. Don't forget a headlamp, extra layers, and to check the actual time of sunrise the night before. Dogs allowed.
8.1-mile loop, moderate–strenuous, 2,283 feet elevation gain

Other Recreational Opportunities

- Take a swim at Sand Beach
- Drive the Park Loop Road

STOP #3: MOUNT WASHINGTON, NEW HAMPSHIRE

Mount Washington holds so many accolades, it would be a mistake not to visit and hike in the incredible Mount Washington State Park. This mountain is the tallest in the northeastern United States at 6,288 feet, and the most prominent mountain east of the Mississippi. If we want to dive deep into Mount Washington fun facts, the mountain holds the record for highest measured wind speed not associated with a tornado or cyclone—a whopping 231 miles per hour. If you plan on visiting, buckle up for some intense climbs, dizzying weather, and a whole lot of beautiful views.

Camping Information

There's plentiful free camping in this area. Pull up your favorite camp-finding app, and go to town, ahem, to a primitive campsite.

Three Ways to Get to the Top

- Ride the Mount Washington Cog Railway. The first mountain-climbing railway of its kind will transport you from the base of the mountain to the summit in around three hours. This isn't the most physically exhausting or environmentally friendly way to get to the top, but you can rest easy by purchasing a trip fueled by biodiesel. Tickets range from ~$40 to $80 per trip.
- Drive the van. From May through October you can drive yourself up through four different climate zones and end up at the summit.
- Use your legs. This is by far the most strenuous of the options, but it's also the most rewarding. With a visitor center at the top, you know you can grab a few treats and a pin to commemorate the tough climb. Expect changing weather conditions (cold and windy), uphill scrambling, and cute dogs. Give yourself plenty of time, and leave early to try to carve out the best weather window.

11.4 miles, strenuous, 4,465 feet elevation gain

Other Recreational Opportunities

- Explore the White Mountain huts of New Hampshire.
- Canoe and fish in one of the many rivers—try Swift for fly fishing and Saco for a canoe trip.
- Downhill mountain or cross-country bike at Loon Mountain.
- As you head toward Portland, Maine, route your house on wheels down the Kancamagus Scenic Byway, from Lincoln to Conway.

STOP #4: PORTLAND, MAINE

If there was ever a place to gorge yourself on seafood, it is in this adorable town. The cobblestone streets and wharf provide the perfect place to take a break from the van, treat yourself to a lobster roll, and then treat yourself to a second lobster roll. Your stomach and wallet might be sad, but your tastebuds will thank you.

Camping Information

While there aren't many free spots to camp right in the city, you can combine a visit to the LL Bean Flagship store (exciting!) twenty minutes outside the city with an overnight stay. LL Bean allows you to park overnight in a posted RV parking area.

Suggested Hike

MACKWORTH ISLAND HIKING TRAIL: Circumnavigate Mackworth Island! This hike offers mostly ocean views and is a good option for people of all skill levels. You'll have the opportunity to see a lot of wildlife and relax to the sound of the waves.
1.4 miles, easy, 45 feet elevation gain

OTHER RECREATIONAL OPPORTUNITIES

- Kayak around Casco Bay and explore the islands
- Mountain bike the Evergreen Cemetery Trails

STOP #5: PROVINCETOWN, MASSACHUSETTS

The Provincetown area and what is now the Cape Cod National Seashore have long been a source for inspiration for creative minds like Henry David Thoreau. Today, much of this area is managed by the National Park Service and is an excellent destination for hiking, biking, swimming, fishing, and surfing. These coastal waters have become an epicenter of great white shark activity and you need to be aware when swimming in the ocean.

Camping Information

While the National Park Service doesn't operate any campgrounds in the park, they do offer vacation cabin rentals. There are also a number of private campgrounds located throughout the island with great access to Provincetown and the park. You won't be able to find free camping in this area.

Suggested Hike

THE GREAT ISLAND TRAIL: This is considered the park's most difficult trail because much of the "trail" is actually just sand. You'll hike through beautiful forests, marshes, and beaches.
4.7-mile loop, moderate, 46 feet elevation gain

Other Recreational Opportunities

- View sandy dunes, wooded forests, and cranberry bogs on the Province Lands Bike Trail.
- Surf! You can find good surfing spots up and down the cape with varying levels of access.

STOP #6: SHAWANGUNK MOUNTAINS, NEW YORK

The Shawangunk Mountains, commonly referred to as the Gunks, are actually the northern part of a long ridge within the Appalachian Mountains. The Gunks are known for their biodiversity but also as an outdoor playground and an adventurer's paradise. These mountains are only located about eighty miles from New York City, but you'd never know it. This area has emerged as one of the top rock-climbing destinations in the country. Don't climb? Have no fear! There are plenty of other opportunities to get out and enjoy this area.

Camping Information

The American Alpine Club cooperatively manages a campground with the Mohonk Preserve. It's called the Samuel F. Pryor III Shawangunk Gateway Campground and is located near the Peterskill climbing area. If you are an AAC member, you can book a site for $24 per night. Otherwise, sites are $38 per night. You can find free boondocking in Sundown Wild Forest not too far from Minnewaska State Park. However, keep in mind this area is close to New York City and can get busy on weekends (GPS: N41.921047' / W74.391174').

Suggested Hikes

GERTRUDE'S NOSE TRAIL IN MINNEWASKA STATE PARK PRESERVE: A diverse hike featuring a large rock outcropping and big views.
7.8 miles, moderate, 1,187 feet elevation gain
BLUE BERRY PASS TO CASTLE POINT TO RAINBOW FALLS LOOP: A scenic day hike that is quieter and more secluded than the other trails in the area.
11.1 miles, moderate, 1,318 feet elevation gain

Suggested Backpacking Route

THE SHAWANGUNK RIDGE TRAIL: A point-to-point trail that traverses the Shawangunk Ridge. You can hike the trail as an out-and-back and go for as long as you'd like. Or you can thru-hike the entire trail, but you'll need to set up a shuttle.
67.1 miles, strenuous, 9,064 feet elevation gain

Other Recreational Opportunities

- Rock climbing. The Gunks are home to several climbing areas and some of the best climbing in the country.

STOP #7: DEEP CREEK LAKE, MARYLAND

Tucked between West Virginia and Pennsylvania is a bunch of potential for adventure. You can finish off your road trip here, but there's so much more to explore (both before this final destination and after). If you're feeling adventurous, pick up the start of the previous road trip in Shenandoah, and make it a full East Coast exploration. Grab a sandwich from The MoonShadow and get to planning!

Camping Information

Just like a few other stops on this trip, you might be hard-pressed to find a nice *free* place to sleep that is also close by. There are plenty of state parks in the area with wonderful camping options. If you really want to treat yourself, book a cabin at Blue Moon Rising and keep the tiny house/eco-friendly vibe going.

Suggested Hike

RHODODENDRON TRAIL TO RIDGE TRAIL TO RATTLESNAKE LOOP: This is a fun loop in Coopers Rock State Forest, West Virginia. Wind your way through unique rock formations, and once you enter "Rock City," you'll find yourself in a wondrous Northeast slot canyon. In the fall the colors are gorgeous.
4.3 miles, moderate, 764 feet elevation gain

Other Recreational Opportunities

- Sail, stand-up paddleboard, kayak, or canoe on Deep Creek Lake.
- Mountain bike at Big Bear Lake Trail Center.
- Whitewater raft or kayak the "Upper Yough" or "Top Yough," two intense sections of the Youghiogheny River—not for the fainthearted.
- Hike or backpack at Dolly Sods Wilderness in Monongahela National Forest.

chapter 13 STAY CONNECTED AND KEEP ON KEEPIN' ON

BUILD YOUR COMMUNITY

LOSS OF COMMUNITY IS OUR BIGGEST HURDLE to van life. This obstacle is followed closely by the inability to partake in repeating activities that involve the same people or teams (instrument lessons, band practice, intramural sports), and finally, the ache of seeing our friends' and families' lives continuing on and missing events and gatherings. Birthday parties, weekend picnics, and camping trips all get viewed secondhand on social media or from later communication. Everyone is building relationships and sharing memories, while you are off adventuring.

Building a community on the road is pivotal to making it work long-term. Without a friendly face every once in a while, the sights get blurred and the freedom gets stale. We are built to live in small close-knit communities and to lean on one another for emotional support. We are most satisfied when we share food, help another with a flat tire, and pull up another chair around the communal campfire. Our nomadic ancestors traveled in supportive communities, and we should strive to mirror that in order to continue traveling for an extended period of time.

WHERE TO TURN

Luckily, in this fully internet-saturated era, if you have a smartphone, you have a portal into many communities. Hopefully, those online comments and likes turn into real-life buddies and besties. Remember, nothing beats face-to-face human connections. But if loneliness strikes and you have cell service, jump online and reach out! Or better yet, call a friend. Call your mom! Call the new hiking buddy you just met! Texting is great, but having a real human voice on the other end of the line can lift you up and soothe the inevitable loneliness of living without roots.

Facebook Groups

There is a Facebook group for everything! You can get as broad and sweeping or as detailed and specific as you'd like. Want help converting your van, specifically a ProMaster? There's a group for that. Want to purchase a Class B camper van? There's a group for that as well. Want general knowledge or just to get the flavor of a van life group? There are multiple groups for that. Figure out what you're interested in, join, and start commenting or posting. Soon, you will see the same names popping up. The community is small. Facebook groups are the easiest way to start your research and get to know a community. There's no cost (except that of an internet-connected device and Wi-Fi), and you can get any question you have answered relatively quickly and with many differing points of view.

Diversify Van Life

This website and Instagram page is a collection of travelers "creating a safe space for BIPOC and underrepresented individuals in the nomadic community . . . created to intentionally celebrate and empower road travelers and outdoorists living at the intersections and taking up space in the margins." It has a wealth of resources, informational online community gatherings, and a monthly magazine.

Van Life Gatherings and Festivals

If you are new to van life, festivals and gatherings are a great way to get to know other nomadic travelers. For endless miles on the road, you are alone, traveling drawn-out roads through shaded forest and cloudy skies. And then you pull into a festival full of like-minded people and the leaves are lifted and the sun seems just right. These van life

MICAH PULLEYN

BREN PHOTOGRAPHY

MICAH PULLEYN IS THE FOUNDER and director of the Asheville Van Life Gathering. It has grown from a happy hour to a freestanding event after only two years. It was the community and the festival's sponsors who really urged Micah to keep the festival going. It was at that point when she thought, "Damn, I've got a really good thing going here, and it's not about me, it's about the community of people."

VEHICLE
2020 Ram ProMaster

CONNECT
@ashevillevanlife

TIME ON ROAD
Part-time, 6 years

COMMUNITY ON THE ROAD
My favorite things about this community include the authenticity of the people, the celebration of adventure and travel, and the sharing of stories and ideas. I am constantly inspired by the people in the van life community. They build endless collective creativity, including storytelling from epic, diverse adventures. People in the van life community also tend to be very genuine, kind, generous, open, and conscientious. I feel like there is a great sense of connection and fellowship when we gather, especially considering how many folks live on the road solo or as couples. I've known so many festivalgoers who form lasting, close friendships at these gatherings.

WORDS OF WISDOM
When in-person is not an option, I prefer to talk on the phone with my fellow van lifers, with some "campfire" video calls (yes, I have hosted a few Zoom calls from my fire pit). I also have picked up the pen and paper and started writing handwritten love notes.

I would love to see the community become more accepting and understanding of the need for diversity, and for van lifers to advocate more for environmental conservation and stewardship.

gatherings always help us to feel a little less crazy. Even traveling as a couple, we are lonely together. It took years for our family and friends to stop asking when this "phase" would be over. When would we be "home" for good? When we got to spend a weekend with other like-minded individuals, we were home for good. And we were reminded that it's all worth it.

Many times you meet new people at these festivals and travel with them for days or weeks afterward. Or you might plan to meet up with a new group in a few weeks' or months' time. Or at the next festival! Seeing a familiar face on the road can brighten any day.

VAN LIFE APPS TO KEEP YOU ROLLING

Applications are a great way to connect with the nomadic community. There are camping apps, local recreation apps, and community-centered apps. The apps we use the most are centered around finding camping. We switch between freecampsites.net, iOverlander, and Google Maps multiple times before deciding on a spot to camp.

Road Trippers

This is a great app to find weird and interesting stopping points along your journey. Nothing lightens a road trip like seeing Carhenge outside Alliance, Nebraska, or Flintstones Bedrock City in Coconino County, Arizona. Though it also suggests gas stations and less exotic pit stops, it's a great resource to find something new along the way.

Wi-Fi Map

Wow, we wish we would have had this app years ago. Wi-Fi Map highlights hot spots nearby, both for open networks and password-protected networks. For networks that are password protected, it shows suggested passwords and when those passwords were last successful. It also lists download and upload speeds for some networks. You can use this app for free with ads, or pay a yearly subscription to remove ads and get a few more bells and whistles. We've had mixed success, sometimes finding hotspot gold mines and sometimes striking out multiple times.

Yelp

Yelp is a great way to find places to eat in new areas, especially for those with dietary restrictions. We use the comment search on particular postings to see if anyone has mentioned "gluten-free" for a bagel shop or "dairy-free" for an ice cream shop and go from there.

The Vanlife App

Community *and* resources. The Vanlife App marries a lot of apps into one, with the added bonus of a lot of community focus. They have virtual meet-ups focused on van topics, van forums, and camping suggestions, and are the same people who put on Vanlife Gatherings throughout the United States. There are paid and free versions of the app.

Flush

While we always thought it was a great "toilet hack" to use the bathrooms in hotel lobbies because they're extremely clean and never busy, this app takes it a step further. Flush boasts a directory of "tens of thousands of public toilets" so you can easily find a comfortable place for your tush on the way to your next destination.

Open Signal

Open Signal has two functions that are super-important to getting work done and plugging in to find community. The first is a speed test. If you upload or download video, large photos, or long audio files, it is important to know the speed of the internet you're currently working on. OpenSignal gives you a fast, easily accessible speed test. This app is also useful for finding out if you will have cell service at your next campsite, or how far you'll need to drive to find a signal. The app uses readings from other users to analyze cell phone signal strength for many different networks.

KEEPING YOUR CLOSE-KNIT COMMUNITY

The loss of community can be challenging, but it doesn't have to be a deal-breaker. Our best advice is to not lose touch with the community you have now. Use van life as an excuse to visit your friends and family all over the country. It's a great way to stay in touch, get a shower, and maybe even do a little laundry. If there are people you can't visit, make a phone call and have actual conversations. You'll have plenty of time while you're on the road. Spoken words are more meaningful than text messages. Making friends is hard, especially as an adult, so keeping the relationships that you cherish should be a main priority.

PROTIP

Plan, dive in, and smile. First, really think it through: How are you going to make a living? How do you want to spend your days? How are you going to educate the kids? How are you going to manage affairs at home base? Next, forget it all and start doing. There is an insurmountable mountain of bullshit in between you and this lifestyle—and once you finally hit the road, it still exists. So the final piece of advice is to smile through it—enjoy the process of creating a life that few others are bold enough to do. **—COLIN BOYD & SOFI ALDINIO**

WHERE TO GO FROM HERE

Throughout this guidebook, we've supplied essentials for how to get out the door and start an alternative lifestyle. But what about when you're halfway through your dream? Or you made it to the Grand Canyon and don't know where to go next? What if you're three months in and the money runs out or the loneliness kicks in? All of these things will happen, maybe at three months or maybe at three years. At some point the shiny dream will become a little duller, and the benefits of fixed plumbing will become painfully obvious. Use the words from van lifers throughout this book to keep you inspired, encourage you to find your next horizon, and remember why you jumped into this crazy lifestyle in the first place.

Variety, as they say, is the spice of life. It's also a cornerstone of van life. Every day will be different and every night of sleep will be a little more interesting. That said, make sure variety infiltrates your overall traveling trends as well. If you're driving a few hours a day and finding a campsite before every sunset, maybe set down for a few weeks outside a small town or city. If you've overstayed your welcome in your friend's driveway after three

---

PROTIP

I think that with a good mindset, just about anywhere can be the best place to visit. Treat it like the grand adventure it is and you'll find treasure everywhere. —KATYA

weeks (we've all been there, we respectfully call it "moochdocking"), then head off into the distance for a few days so everyone can have some breathing room. If you've spent every winter chasing waves in Baja, try Arizona or Utah for something new. If you're feeling especially spicy, head north and see what cold-weather van life is all about! Make sure to do the scary things, turn left when you usually go right, and visit that friend you haven't seen in ten years.

Eventually, the loneliness will seep in, even as partners traveling. Always call a friend, head to a van life gathering, or stop back by your home base. After a few months, the loneliness will be replaced with new friendships, favorite camp spots, and a traveling community. Lean into it.

There is always the chance that you run into a huge engine repair, or van life was far

DANI REYES-ACOSTA

KAYA LINDSAY

DANI STARTED LIVING ON THE ROAD six years ago without any prior knowledge of van life. What later became a process of becoming (i.e., finding herself through adventuring) started as a recognition that it wouldn't be feasible for her—a solo woman traveler—to haul four seasons of gear around a foreign country using public transportation.

VEHICLE + WHY
1995 Ford E250 RWD—I chose this vehicle purely out of a need to replace my broken truck—"right place at the right time."

CONNECT
@NotLostJustDiscovering

TIME ON THE ROAD
Full- and part-time, 6 years

WORDS OF WISDOM
As more people enter the outdoors, many shifting away from deskbound, tethered lifestyles, we must temper the rugged individualism marking our cultural attitudes. With the growth of van life and proliferation of individual, self-sufficient islands of perfection, I've observed and experienced careless, reckless attitudes and behaviors that disregard others as often as I've experienced welcoming, warm community.

I'm optimistic that more of us will see how we're united by the land that supports us. I'm optimistic more of us will begin to actively steward the land and build links to the tethered communities adjacent to the lands where we live and play.

more expensive than you initially estimated. Use chapter 6 to find other forms of revenue. Pivot from what you're currently doing to try something new. Don't be ashamed of staying in a friend's or family member's driveway to get your bearings straight and have solid internet for a few days. You can do this!

Ultimately, van life is hard. There is no way around it, no shortcut, no bypass. It is a rough lifestyle. But the rewards far outweigh the tribulations, and there is a community waiting with open arms to help you along the entire way. Reach out to us (really!), or van life Instagram accounts, or forums—community is your greatest asset. Be kind to the land, be kind to the communities you pass through, be open for adventure as well as misadventure. Enjoy!

chapter 14 CHECKLISTS TO GET YOU STARTED

WHAT YOU DECIDE TO PACK will come down to what you want, need, and have space for in your new home. We hit the road so we could spend more time in the great outdoors, not so we could spend a lot of time in our van! With this in mind during our build-out, we sacrificed livable space on the inside of our van for lots of storage. We wanted to bring all of our outdoor gear along with the household items we use on a regular basis. Your checklist will probably be very different than ours, but our sample packing list will give you ideas for what you might want to bring along on your adventure. Try to avoid bringing too many "just in case" items. We had a giant inflatable slice of pizza "just in case" we had the urge to go for a float on a nearby waterway. While we did use it, and it was amazing, it probably wasn't worth the space it took up—sorry pizza.

GENERAL PACKING CHECKLIST

- ❍ Toilet paper
- ❍ Toiletries
    - ❍ Toothbrush
    - ❍ Toothpaste
    - ❍ Floss
    - ❍ Biodegradable soap
    - ❍ Shampoo and conditioner
    - ❍ Hand sanitizer
- ❍ Bug spray
- ❍ Sunscreen
- ❍ First-aid kit
- ❍ Solar shower
- ❍ Towels
- ❍ Extra sheets
- ❍ All outdoor gear (backpacking, camping, mountain biking, climbing, fishing, etc.)
- ❍ Appropriate clothing and outerwear
- ❍ Bathing suit
- ❍ Appropriate footwear (sandals, boots, climbing shoes, etc.)
- ❍ Entertainment (tablet, books, e-reader, etc.)
- ❍ Extension cord
- ❍ Laptops and chargers
- ❍ Water bottles
- ❍ Thermoses
- ❍ Maps
- ❍ Personal locator beacon and GPS
- ❍ Camera gear
- ❍ Bike rack
- ❍ Flashlights and headlamps
- ❍ Tire levels
- ❍ Jumper cables
- ❍ Tow strap

- ○ Air compressor
- ○ Shovel
- ○ Hatchet
- ○ Fire starter
- ○ Fire extinguisher
- ○ Tool kit
- ○ Pocket knife/multitool
- ○ Doormat

KITCHEN PACKING CHECKLIST

- ○ Food
- ○ Water
- ○ Coffee (beans, grinder, French press, mugs)
- ○ Plates
- ○ Bowls
- ○ Cups
- ○ Cutting board
- ○ Cast irons
- ○ Collapsible pot w/strainer lid
- ○ Two-burner stove
- ○ Jetboil (backpacking stove)
- ○ Fuel (propane and isobutane)
- ○ Instant pot
- ○ Toaster
- ○ Silverware + sharp knife
- ○ Spatula
- ○ Bottle opener/wine opener
- ○ Can opener
- ○ Biodegradable trash bags
- ○ Reusable rags
- ○ Salt + pepper, favorite spices

KITCHEN EXTRAS

- ○ Extra pots and pans
- ○ Peeler
- ○ Strainer
- ○ Wineglasses
- ○ Measuring cups

WINTER PACKING LIST

- ○ Tire chains
- ○ Kitty litter (in case you get stuck)
- ○ Snow scraper
- ○ Shovel
- ○ Water tank heaters
- ○ Oil pan heater
- ○ Winter clothes
- ○ Winter footwear
- ○ Extra blankets
- ○ Winter outdoor gear
- ○ Extra windshield wiper fluid

PACKING LIST FOR PET OWNERS

- ○ Pet (important)
- ○ Pet bed
- ○ Food and water bowls
- ○ Collapsible water bowl (for hiking)
- ○ Brush (for brushing out all of those brambles they just ran through)
- ○ Leash (plus an extra because someone keeps losing them)
- ○ Light-up nighttime collar
- ○ Collar and tags (with up-to-date contact information)
- ○ Vet records (can be digital)
- ○ Treats (always)
- ○ Reflective vest
- ○ Evaporative cooling vest

- ○ Pet trimmers or scissors
- ○ Flea and tick collar
- ○ Heartworm medication
- ○ Poop bags
- ○ Towel

VEHICLE MAINTENANCE CHECKLIST

- ○ Oil change
- ○ Tire inspection (including tire pressure and tread depth)
- ○ Check fluid levels
- ○ Check lights and turn signals
- ○ Check for up-to-date registration (make sure it will be valid for the duration of your trip)
- ○ Check air filter
- ○ Spare tire and jack
- ○ Battery life/jumper cables
- ○ Check auxiliary power/solar
- ○ Check all plumbing for leaks
- ○ Clean vent fan

LIVING BUDGET WORKSHEET

Here is an empty chart to get you started on an estimate of monthly expenses or to track your expenses on the road. Go for it, fill it out! Even if it's just guessing, it will be helpful information to get you moving toward your goal.

OUTGOING MONEY—VAN	NOTES	COST
Automobile insurance		
Van payment (if purchased new)		
Build-out payment (if a third party was used)		
Gas		
Maintenance		
Other		
OUTGOING MONEY—PERSONAL		
Health Insurance		
Groceries/alcohol/eating out		
Water and/or ice		
Campgrounds		
Experiences		
Telephone and internet		
Laundry		
Gym membership and showers		
Entertainment subscriptions		
Gifts/clothing/gear		
Toll roads		
Emergency		
Storage (if you have any)		
AAA coverage		
Pet supplies and food		
	Total monthly expenses:	

ABOUT THE AUTHORS

ROXY AND BEN left their east coast home states and found each other in the front range of Colorado in 2015. They've been exploring the corners of the United States and abroad from the comfort of a van since 2017. They've scrambled on the lava rock of Iceland, back-country snowboarded on volcanos in Japan, trekked to high alpine huts in New Zealand, and reflected among old-growth trees on the coast of Canada, all with a van as a home base to return to each exhausted evening. Roxy and Ben now live part-time in the van and part-time in Golden, Colorado, spending their days writing, cuddling their beloved and scruffy pup, Henry, and planning the next big adventure. You can find updates on their travels, their recent work, and hopefully some inspiration on their website, benthere roxythat.com.